MY SEA LADY

MY SEA LADY

HMS *Lady Madeleine*

February 1941 to February 1943

GRAEME OGDEN

BENE FACTUM PUBLISHING

My Sea Lady

This edition published in 2013 by
Bene Factum Publishing Ltd
PO Box 58122
London
SW8 5WZ

Email: inquiries@bene-factum.co.uk
www.bene-factum.co.uk

ISBN: 978-1-903657-17-5
Text © The Estate of the late Graeme Ogden

With kind permission of the heirs of the late Graeme Ogden's estate, this edition
has been published to mark the 2013 award of the Arctic Star to the veterans of
the Russian Arctic convoys.
Any royalties received by the estate in respect of sales will be donated to the
Russian Arctic Convoy Museum [Registered charity number SC042286].

A CIP catalogue record of this is available from the British Library.

Illustrations by Richard Elsden
Typesetting by Carnegie Book Production
Cover by Ian Hughes of Mousemat Design Ltd
Printed in the UK

CONTENTS

INTRODUCTION

by
Alan Ogden

In 1945 my father, Graeme Ogden, was hospitalised in New York with a recurrent stomach disorder he had contracted in Murmansk in 1943 when escorting convoys to Russia. A beautiful 21-year-old girl from North Carolina came on a hospital visit to see him, her way of helping the war effort. His own marriage over, my father fell head over heels in love with her and soon after my sister and I were born in quick succession.

Growing up in the 1950s, I watched an endless stream of films about heroic British officers including naval epics such as *Sink the Bismark*, *The Battle of the River Plate*, *Dunkirk* and *The Cruel Sea*. Naturally my father became such a hero to me although he never discussed his wartime service, however much I pestered him. So I had to limit my admiration to writing letters to him from boarding school, addressed to Lieutenant Commander W.G. Ogden, DSC, RNVR. Since this line went right across the top of the envelope, I felt extremely proud of him.

Several years later, I remember coming home one school holiday and finding him writing a manuscript by hand. He was rather protective about it and so I didn't pry. Vast quantities of cigarettes were consumed, reams of paper scrunched up, until the great day when *My Sea Lady* appeared as a hardback book in the window of John Sandoe's bookshop in Chelsea. Various other manuscripts were subsequently crafted, usually thrillers, but sadly none saw the light of day.

When I learnt that the British government had decided to recognise the self-sacrifice and gallantry of all those involved in the Arctic convoys, it seemed an opportune moment to read *My Sea Lady* again, this time with the benefit of life experience rather than schoolboy adulation.

What strikes me is the honesty of his account. He hated war, the waste of precious time, the waste of life and waste of resources. He had to close his successful electronics business which employed German technicians, his marriage came unstuck and he lost several close friends. He watched men die in appalling circumstances, risking his life and that of his crew on many occasions to try and save them.

Yet the war made him a more compassionate human being rather than a desensitised one. It helped him put a value on what was important and what was not. Undoubtedly he relished the responsibilities and duties of commanding a small ship and was devoted to his crew. Strangely, after becoming such an accomplished sailor, he rarely took us sailing, preferring the peace and quiet of fly fishing.

That said, my father had his wartime demons to battle with. He vanquished them through self-reflection and faith in his fellow men and God. *My Sea Lady* was very much part of that fight.

Any profit which accrues as a result of sales of this edition will be donated to the Russian Arctic Convoys Museum project at Loch Ewe, which will hopefully be home to a permanent memorial to all those who served.

My father, who passed away some thirty years ago, would have been immensely proud to wear the Arctic Star; I am honoured to accept it in his memory.

Alan Ogden, June 2013

FOREWORD

by
Rear-Admiral Rupert Sherbrook,
VC, CB, DSO, DL, JP

Dear Graeme,

I have read your manuscript with the greatest interest. You have recorded your experiences in a way that is perhaps not possible in more formal histories, and, while not departing from the authenticity of events, by your personal reactions you have added an outstanding account of the human factors which are ultimately so important.

The small ships shepherded the convoys often under appalling conditions of wind, ice and mountainous seas. For those onboard there was frequently little eatable food and they were usually wet through even when below decks.

I pay tribute to you all as a grand lot of seafarers who added a magnificent chapter in the history of the Royal Navy.

Very sincerely yours,

Rupert Sherbrooke

Oxton, Nottinghamshire
(1963)

PREFACE

by
THE AUTHOR

This story was written in its original form in the latter part of 1943 when the author was convalescing from 'battle fatigue'. The chances of its ever being published were remote in the extreme, as when the author went back to sea next year the manuscript and the diaries from which it had been compiled were, to all intents and purposes, lost forever.

These came back into the author's possession seventeen years later in the most unexpected and extraordinary way. They had, in fact, been left by the author in his mother's country house and been tidied away into the bottom drawer of a chest of drawers, and it was not until her death that the papers came to light. Even then the chances of their survival were unlikely, for the chest of drawers was left to the author's daughter, who threw the papers into a dustbin; but kept one or two photographs. These happened to be seen by her father a day or two later, who asked where they had come from. On being told, he remembered the book which he had long ago given up as lost, so he immediately organized a hectic search through the dustbin, which proved to be successful.

With the diaries and a very battered manuscript back in his possession, the author decided to read the papers out of curiosity. He found them sufficiently entertaining to rewrite the story.

The story is presented here in this form, after various minor alterations being made, such as taking out a great deal of very unparliamentary language and so on. The rest of it remains as in the original.

Names of people, ships, places and battles are all as they existed or happened at that time, with only three exceptions. Sally is a mixture of several people and 'Speedy's' name was not Donald and Squires is an invented name. The object of the book is to give the story of the many young men who joined the R.N.V.R. and went to the war at sea in small ships.

To the author, the story of *Lady M*, as you will read it, is not so much the story of a small band of men flung together by circumstances out of their own control, who fought together for two years, but rather the story of the humanities concerned.

In essence, this story should not fall into the category of most war reminiscences and autobiographies, because it was written in 1943 as an emotional reaction to a tough and unexpected war at sea by a person who, at that period, did not try to hide his feelings – at least, not very successfully.

The book is in truth an epitaph to those of us who, twenty years ago, set off to the wars and to those of us who returned sickened and dispirited by the futility of a now meaningless crusade.

If, by accident, the author has inadvertently caused anybody mentioned in the book any embarrassment or offence he would like to apologize immediately and say that his impressions gathered seventeen years ago may easily have been out of focus and also incorrect.

GRAEME OGDEN
73 Eaton Square
London, S.W.1
(1963)

BOOK ONE

THE NARRATIVE

On a cold blustery morning in February 1941 I picked my way through the Belfast dockyard in search of the ship I was to command.

I was looking for H.M.S. *Lady Madeleine*—Fishery No. 183—an ocean-going fishing trawler, which had been converted for anti-submarine duties. According to my instructions she was lying alongside the sea-wall in berth No. 11, having undergone a refit. She was scheduled to be 'in all respects ready for sea' within the next day or two.

A dockyard is usually a most depressing place, cluttered up with old boilers, rust wires and all the flotsam and jetsam that has accumulated there over the years, but on this occasion it was for me the most exciting place in the world. I quickened my step as I peered through the maze of ships' masts.

When at last I found *Lady M* my heart sank, and (as their Lordships would say) I viewed the situation 'with grave concern'. The ship which was to be my first command resembled a smouldering scrap-heap.

I fought my way through the milling crowd of dockyard maties and gained the lower bridge. The view from here was appalling. The decks were littered with oxyacetylene welding equipment, de-gaussing gear, lengths of rusty anchor cable, firebars and heaven knows that else. The upper, or asdic, bridge, which was being reconstructed, contained a tangle of wires and electrical equipment. Outside, the noise of rivets being driven home was so deafening that I didn't hear Brian Westwood come in and introduce himself. Brian was to be my first lieutenant and had served in *Lady M* under her previous captain. He told me that the crew were due to return from leave the following day.

After exchanging a few pleasantries and eyeing each other rather nervously, we went down to the C.O's cabin to await the arrival of Lieutenant Potter, R.N.R., the ship's former commanding officer. In the meanwhile I inspected my new home. In peacetime a trawler skipper's quarters are very comfortable compared with most small ships, as trawler owners wish to attract the most successful men available. The cabin contained a bunk with drawers under it, a desk, a chart-table, easy chair, sofa, bookshelves and a bottle-and-glass rack. The furniture was of polished mahogany and the steel bulkheads were painted white. There was a small bathroom aft—on the starboard side. The method of heating the water was to full up with cold sea-water and then blow a jet of boiling steam into it.

Westwood and I sat down on the sofa and began to yarn. The atmosphere in the cabin was moist, stagnant and cold, owing to the port-holes having been secured for the past few weeks and the ship's boilers being out. We decided to light the bogey and also to let some air into the place.

I gathered from Brian that *Lady Madeleine* had been commissioned at Harwich on 25th May 1940. Later on, when I got to know her better, I always regarded this date as her birthday, and here is her birth certificate:

CONFIDENTIAL

COMMISSIONING ORDER

MEMORANDUM

The Lords Commissioners of the Admiralty having directed that His Majesty's Ship *Lady Madeleine* is to be commissioned on Saturday the 25th May, 1940, with a Naval crew, for service as A/S Trawler at HARWICH, with accounts carried out in *Badger*, you are to proceed to commission this vessel, and to cause the utmost despatch to be used, so far as the same may depend on you, in preparing for sea accordingly.

Given under my hand at Hull, this 25th day of May, 1940.

Rear-Admiral Flag Officer Humber.

To Lieut. Comdr. T.G. Hill, R.N.R., Commanding Officer H.M.T. *Lady Madeleine*.

Copies to: Secretary of the Admiralty Commander-in-Chief, The Nore, Belfast.

Brian also told me she was a Hull-built ship, and one of the largest ocean-going trawlers afloat. I noticed the 'afloat' reference, as I knew her sister ship *Lady Elsa* had been attacked and sunk by a long-range German aircraft two weeks before.

I learned that *Lady M* was 195 ft. long, with a beam of 32 ft. and a draught of 18 ft. 6 in. Her hull was constructed of ¾ in. riveted steel plates, and her underwater section was as graceful as a yacht's. Her engines were of the ripple expansion 'up and down' type and fed by two boilers. When the steam pressure was up she could do nearly 14 knots. She had been provided by her designers with very large coal-bunkers, as originally she had been intended for fishing in distant waters. I was to discover later on that we could stay at sea for a month or more. We had, in fact, a cruising range of some three thousand miles without re-fuelling or taking in water.

Our conversation was interrupted by the arrival of Lieutenant Potter, who looked every inch a seaman, with his blue eyes and ginger beard. Without waiting for any formalities the three of us toasted *Lady M* and drank to the success of my command. We talked about trawlers for a while, and Potter praised their sea-going qualities, and also warned me of some of their bad habits. He then handed over the ship's papers, gave me the key of the safe and took his leave. I intimated to Brian I should like to be left alone. It was about 1300. The shipwrights had knocked off for lunch and the din had subsided. I lit a cigarette and sat down at my desk to think. True enough, I had served in two other anti-submarine trawlers as No.1 and No.2, but to be in command of a ship, however small and insignificant, filled me with uneasiness. I was only an amateur at the best of times, and now I had the full responsibility of *Lady M* and her complement of some forty souls.

We were to be engaged in protecting and escorting valuable merchant shipping. I had very little experience to guide me, and after smoking several cigarettes I came to the conclusion that my own fate and that of *Lady M*, her officers and crew, depended on how fast I could learn my new trade. I went ashore, had some food and then drew a boiler-suit from the N.S.O. I put this on and spent the afternoon exploring my ship.

A ship with her boilers blown down is a miserable and clammy place. The shore lighting is insufficient, and the very atmosphere is depressing. There appeared to be nothing but grease and grime wherever I penetrated and the stale smell of coal and engine oil.

In 1940 Belfast was the main trawler base for Western Approaches Command. This was before the days of the mass-produced corvettes, and the ocean-going trawlers were collected there and fitted out according to what gear was available, rather than to any standard specification. A 'refit' could mean almost anything.

Later that afternoon, when I had finished my inspection, I considered that in the circumstances we were not too badly off. We had a primitive asdic apparatus, a modern 4 in. gun forward, a twin ½ in. Vickers machine gun aft, two Lewis guns on the bridge, a port and starboard depth-charge thrower and a D/C rack over the stern.

In the evening, after a solitary supper, I moved my gear aboard *Lady M* and stowed it away. I also checked the contents of the ship's safe. Over my bunk there was a brass oil-lamp swung on gimbles. Its design struck me as the sort of thing one might see in one of Manet's pictures of the Paris music-halls. To this I attached my talisman, a silver slipper which Sally had given me for luck. After this I turned in.

H uddled beneath my overcoat with my gasmask for a pillow, I shivered with cold. I was not to know on that first night aboard *Lady M* that we were going to be inseparable companions for the next two years.

I did not realize then that a ship and her complement are bound together with the ties of life and death and that perhaps in no other sphere of the war were men so dependent on one another and upon the ship in which they served.

We in *Lady M* would be at sea for weeks on end, usually in the Atlantic, but sometimes in southern waters or the Arctic. Our world was small and unique. We were fighting to save the merchant ships from the ravages of U-boats and the bombs of marauding German aircraft. In the course of the next two years we were to make many lone ocean passages. It was then that I became obsessed with an appalling sense of loneliness. By day we sailed beneath the huge dome of the sky. At night the remoteness of the stars made our very existence seem absurd. Dawns would find us bleary-eyed and convinced that if we did not sight land or see another ship we would sail into oblivion. A ship's wartime routine can be very monotonous.

At sea the ship's bell is struck every half-hour, and the watch changes every four hours. The log is read, tin mugs are filled with cocoa, meals are served. The beat of the ship's propeller remains constant, so does the noise of the wind in the rigging and the slapping of the waves against the ship.

In the asdic cabin the incessant 'ping' goes out from the dome beneath the ship as regularly as the ticking of a clock. Only if it stopped would anybody notice it.

On the bridge the officer of the watch checks the course with the quartermaster in the wheelhouse below. In the engine-room the polished machinery slides up and down, the stokers shovel the coal, the ship sails on.

Tired and uncomfortable as I was that night, sleep would not come to me. My head was filled with the legends of the sea, its fabulous ships and the commanders. I might be very green and inexperienced, I thought to myself, but I was now the commander of an ocean-going ship, so I let myself drift into the realms of fantasy and welcomed the ghosts who invaded my cabin.

*   *   *

'*Toda la noche oyeron pasar pájaros*—surely all these birds must be heading for land?' I looked Columbus straight in the eye and replied quietly, 'We shall see land tomorrow.' This was on 10th October 1492 and the crew of the *Santa Maria* were near to mutiny as we had sailed from Palos in early September. Columbus believed the world to be round, but his crew did not, so he asked me in a loud voice if I was certain we should find Japan. With an inscrutable smile I said firmly, '*Vamos muchachos.*' Next day, the look-out, Rodrigo de Triano, saw the outskirts of the New World. After the

Santa Maria broke up we sailed home in the *Niňa*. I had suggested taking this caravel with us, as her lateen rig was better suited to the beat eastwards. I remembered the *Niňa* was but 70 ft. long and the *Lady M* was 195 ft.

To be held a prisoner aboard an enemy warship is a terrible fate and yet this was my position when the Duke of Medina-Sidonia ordered me to appear before him in his state cabin in the Spanish galleon the *San Marten*. After the Armada this crippled ship had been round Scotland and we were now drifting off Ireland.

I stood in icy silence before him.

'You know these coasts, Captain Ogden,' he said. 'And we are lost and in peril. If you will take over ...'

'*Nunca,*' I spat at him, narrowing my eyes. 'Do your worst with your tortures.'

The Duke handed me a document. I gave it a sneering glance. It was a copy of his letter to King Philip II in which he had written: 'My health is not equal to such a voyage, for I know by experience of the little I have been at sea that I am always seasick and always catch cold. Since I have no experience of the sea or war, I cannot feel that I ought to command so important an enterprise.'

Medina looked at me imploringly.

'I hope you and your ship perish,' I said with a fleeting smile playing around my lips. Then, walking calmly from the cabin, I dived overboard and swam to the Irish coast. Medina would not, I decided, have qualified for the R.N.V.R. in 1939.

Somewhat comforted by the Duke's amateur performance, I thought about the great admirals and explorers who, in their frail ships, had won fabulous battles and conquered the oceans. Drake, Raleigh, Nelson, Vasco da Gama, Magellan, de Torres, Cook, Tasman and Barents.

After rounding Cape Horn, neither Magellan nor I could believe our eyes when we first saw the immensely blue Pacific Ocean with its mile-long swells. Our voyage westwards without seeing land defied description, and when in 1521 he was murdered by the natives of Manila I had taken over command, thus being the first mariner to circumnavigate the globe. This is not confirmed in history but it happened that night in my cabin.

My dreams often turn to sailing ships, as, for me, they have a fascinating beauty and enchantment of their own, and so on this particular night I was not surprised to find myself in East Boston visiting Donald McKay, the builder of the unsurpassed clipper, the *Flying Cloud*.

'You're the best master in sail the British have, I believe?' McKay said to me rather grudgingly.

'Your Captains "Bully" Waterman and "Joe" Cressy are pretty good,' I answered calmly, with a confident smile.

'Well, they're not available for the next trip to China, so I want you to have the command,' McKay said to me in this thick, Scottish accent.

'I should be charmed and delighted,' I answered. And then—

'Crack on the moon sails,' I said quietly to the first mate. Even beneath his weather-beaten skin I saw the blood leave his face. Gazing quizzically aloft at the taut sails stretched almost to breaking point by the fury of the roaring forties, I ordered the helmsman to bring the ship nearer the wind.

'We're out for the record,' I shouted to the seamen as they swarmed up the shrouds. The rest of the crew grinned at one another. If this English captain was going to beat the previous record they were behind him to a man.

Under pressure, the *Flying Cloud* heeled sharply over. Her masts, as high as Nelson's Column, were now at an angle of 45 degrees as she knifed her stream-lined hull through the angry waves. The wind tore through the bar-tight rigging, making it hum like piano wires. A sudden gust struck the ship. Calmly I braced myself against the wheel.

* * *

MY SEA LADY

I landed on the floor of *Lady M*'s cabin with a thud and was lucky not to have done myself any serious injury. I was stiff, cold and miserable. The place was in darkness and as cold as the inside of a refrigerator.

N ext morning I went ashore early; shaved, breakfasted and went to pay my respects to the Flag Officer in charge. The usual waiting-about took place, followed by a stilted conversation with the Admiral, who neither knew nor cared who I was, or what I was supposed to be doing in Belfast. This formality over, I dashed back to H.M.S. *Caroline*, the base ship at Pollock Dock, to enquire what arrangements had been made for my crew, who were due to return from leave, as it was clear that nobody (besides myself) could sleep aboard *Lady M*.

The officer in charge of the trawler base casually enquired who I was! I explained that the Admiralty had appointed me as C.O. of *Lady M*. The base didn't appear to have any trace of such an appointment—and so it went on for hours until it was time for the morning gin session. Then somebody turned up who remembered something about a new C.O. for *Lady M*. I encountered another lost-looking type who turned out to be David Lynx Odham, who had been appointed as No.2 to *Lady M*. We had lunch together, and I discovered he had been at Winchester prior to joining the R.N.V.R. This was fine, but I was a little anxious what effect his appearance would have on the crew, for he sported a beard and a monocle.

We went back to *Lady M*, where Brian met us and introduced us to Bill Sedgewick, who had just joined the ship as No.3. Well, I now had three officers, which was the standard ration in A/S trawlers. The complement of these ships in 1940-1 consisted of the C.O. and three watch-keeping officers, a chief engineer, 'the second' and a coxswain—the last three ranking as petty officers. You had a leading seaman, two asdic operators, 'Sparks' and his assistant wireless stand-in, 'Bunts' the senior signalman, a bosun (if you were lucky), a gunner's mate and two A.A. ratings. The rest of the crew included the ship's cook, stokers, seamen and a wardroom steward.

The first lieutenant's duties were to run the ship's routine, which included victualling and naval stores, the latter covering ammunition, depth-charges and the ship's general equipment. On leaving or approaching harbour, his position was on the fo'c'sle. At action stations he was in charge of the 4 in. gun on the whaleback. No.2 took charge of the depth-charge party aft and was responsible for correcting and keeping up to date the necessary Admiralty charts and navigational information. No.3 was normally in charge of our 'confidential books', which were kept in the ship's office and included codes and recognition signals. At action stations he was in command of the fire brigade or damage-control party. The chief ruled over the engine-room, the coal-bunkers and the fresh-water supply.

As I stood talking to my newly found officers, I felt we should all of us need every ounce of determination we possessed if we were ever going to get *Lady M* to sea. The confusion on her decks was worse than ever. I took comfort in the thought that the present situation might be comparable to a dress rehearsal of a musical play, when in spite of apparently impossible obstacles the show successfully opens on time. Perhaps Sally's silver slipper would bring us luck.

I was most relieved to find that Brian had made the necessary arrangements for the crew and officers to sleep ashore without bothering to notify the trawler base. He thought that we might get the situation under control within a day or two. I thought it most unlikely, but, as I was to find out later, he was a most capable and efficient person.

There is very little a captain can do when his ship is refitting, except keep out of the way, so I tried to put my own affairs in order. I should have been supplied with a sextant, a ship's chronometer, navigational tables, night glasses and a deck watch. I applied at the base for these items in vain, and ended up by buying an assorted selection from a ships' chandler in Belfast.

I spent some time at the officers' club at Pollock Dock and, as a new boy, hung about on the fringe of the other commanding officers. By consuming vast amounts of gin I succeeded in making friends with some of my contemporaries. They seemed incredibly tough, and quite a few were professional peacetime fishing skippers, now R.N.R. trawler captains. These men considered a bottle of whisky or gin an appetizer before setting off for an evening in Belfast town. I tried it once, but never again.

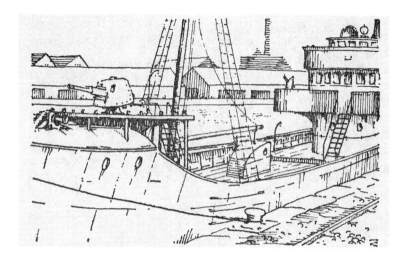

'*M irabile dictu*', within the next two days, Brian had achieved some sort of law and order aboard *Lady M*. The crew kipped down in the mess decks, the chief had flashed up his boilers, the dynamo was working, the galley stove was alight—we had become a community. The wardroom had begun to function. I was able to feed and drink there—things were looking up. The wardroom steward was clearly a 'character', as we shall see later on in this tale. He spoke with a most genteel accent and his opening remark to me was 'With or without, sire?' This referred to water or no water with the gin. I appreciated the 'sire' instead of 'sir'. As we only possessed one steward, this man, whose name was Squires, was also my personal steward.

He was very much the gentleman's gentleman, and one day I asked him, while he was busying himself in my cabin, how he came to be steward in a trawler. Squires replied that he had 'a slight failing...er...the bottle...sire'. The fact that my bottle rack was full, and within reach, immediately became a problem.

'Squires,' I said rather pompously, 'I know how these things are, and I don't wish you to help yourself to my spirits. If you ever feel you simply must have a drink, please ask me, don't pinch one.' Squires' face brightened.

'I'll have a large whisky,' he said, without the least embarrassment.

The arrival of a signal from H.M.S. *Caroline*, informing me that I was to take *Lady M* down-channel next day to carry out engine trials at Bangor Bay, brought me up with a round turn. The time when one sits in the pavilion with one's pads on, watching the other fellows play, was over. Now I had to face the bowling.

I sent for No.1 and enquired if such a venture was possible. The ship had not yet been officially handed back to the Admiralty by the local dockyard, and was still in the hands of the dockyard maties and engineers. We had no coxswain and the chief was far from satisfied with the engines. I discovered afterwards it was his complaints to the base engineering staff that had precipitated this trial. Brian and I, having consulted Whitehead, the chief engineer, decided to 'concur with this order'. I knew I had to break the ice sooner or later and was glad to have to make the decision.

At eleven o'clock next day a tug appeared and pulled *Lady M* away from the dockyard wall and then cast off her lines, leaving us in the middle of Pollock Dock, facing the entrance to the Herdman Channel. 'Midships,' I said down the voice-pipe to the leading seaman on the wheel. This was the first helm order I had ever given as commanding officer, and my heart was in my mouth.

'Midships,' the quartermaster repeated.

'Slow ahead,' I said down the engine-room voice-pipe.

'Slow ahead,' the chief replied in his thick North Country accent. For the first time I heard and felt *Lady M*'s heart begin to beat. We began to gather way, an off-shore wind was taking the ship to starboard.

'Port one turn,' I ordered.

Lady M, going a little faster, did not respond. Not knowing my ship, I thought that perhaps she hadn't enough way on her to answer to the help so I went 'half ahead'. Still she didn't answer me, so I called for hard-a-port. Nothing happened. In a panic I realized the steam steering engine couldn't be working. We were, in fact, a ship without a rudder.

'Full astern,' I yelled to the engine-room. *Lady M* shuddered and stopped a few yards from the other side of the dock. I have never been sick at sea, but I was nearer to it then than ever before. The only other C.O. I know who had a similar experience was a man named Karminski, who gave up the unequal struggle.

The ignominy of being towed back to our berth, watched by my fellow C.O.s, was beyond description. The fact that the dock-yard engineers had forgotten to connect my steering gear was of little comfort as I faced the ribald comments on the inhabitants of Pollock Dock. I did learn one thing, however, and that is the golden rule that every C.O. before 'letting go' should turn over his engines and test his steering gear.

The following day more trouble lay in store for us. This time I succeeded in getting the ship clear of Pollock Dock, but failed to turn sharply enough at the buoys which make the entrance into the Herdman Channel.

We had sailed at nearly low water on an ebb tide, which we should never have been required to do. The result was we went aground and stuck fast in the putty. I knew we would float off at high water, but my anxiety was how much more the tide would fall. If it fell too much we might topple over. I sent away two kedge anchors in the sea-boat and hoped for the best. Four hours later we were afloat again, but our troubles weren't over. The Herdman Channel leads into the Victoria Channel, which is only about 200 ft. wide, and three miles long. It sounds easy enough, but, with an inexperienced helmsman and a high wind, we zig-zagged from one side to the other of this crowded thoroughfare in the most alarming manner. I was very thankful when we returned to harbour without having hit anything.

We spent the next week working up the ship and doing further trials. I was beginning to lose some of my nervousness after such a shaky start. Driving a strange ship is like driving somebody else's car, one just has to get the feel of it before one has any confidence or can take any liberties. In due course a coxswain joined the ship—a strange silent fisherman from Wales whose speech I could hardly understand. Then we were ordered to sail to the Clyde and join the 4th Escort Group. I was glad we were now going to war in earnest, as I was tired of the comic-opera atmosphere which existed in Belfast. H.M.S. *Caroline* might well have been H.M.S. *Pinafore*.

We gave a party in our wardroom and asked one or two other trawler C.O.s and their No.1s. I had made one friend at least and that was Leo Gradwell, who was captain of the trawler *Ayrshire*. We had met in rather a strange way, for one night when returning aboard *Lady M*, as I was climbing over the intervening trawlers, there was a loud crash behind me, and I heard a cultivated voice announce, 'The favourite's down.' I looked round to find a body on the deck of the next ship. This turned out to be Leo, whom I assisted back to his cabin abroad *Ayrshire*. We had some drinks together, and I discovered he was a product of Balliol College, Oxford, and, in peacetime, a barrister on the Northern Circuit. Neither of us knew it at the time, but we were to spend much time in company together, and to go on another type of 'Northern Circuit'. The next day, at daylight, *Lady M* sailed for the Clyde.

I n 1941 the Clyde was chock-a-block with shipping of all descriptions. When we had gone through the boom opposite Dunoon we could see two or three battleships anchored in the roads, towering above a host of merchantmen. After passing Gourock we saw the destroyers riding to their moorings at the Tail of the Bank. Such was the crush that small fry such as trawlers had to tie up the best they could, either at Princes Pier or alongside the outer wall of the Albert Harbour. We had been given a berth at Princes Pier at Greenock, but I had no idea how to find it. After several abortive attempts we found an empty space and tied up. It was daylight, and we had arrived on an ebb tide, so were not faced with the difficulties we were to encounter later on.

The Clyde is tidal at Greenock, and above, and at spring tides the river runs as fast as seven knots. As one must go alongside into the stream, coming home from sea on a flood tide produced some harrowing experiences, it being necessary to turn the ship in this narrow, busy channel. Single-screw ships with slow-revving engines do not turn easily in a confined space by 'backing and filling', as when you go astern the thrust of the right-hand screw makes the ship sheer off to starboard. With a stiff off-shore breeze and the river full of traffic, which might include anything from a battleship coming down from John Brown's yard to hoppers, scoots, drifters and merchantmen, tying up alongside had its problems.

As soon as we had 'secured', I shaved, put on my No.1 uniform and went ashore to report to Captain D. Greenock, under whose command we had been placed.

Captain D's offices were at the back of Albert Harbour and there I found Lieutenant-Commander Davies, R.N.V.R., who was the senior officer in charge of operations (S.O.O.). We were to become great friends later on, but all I noticed at this time was that he wrote with his left hand. Half an hour later I was ushered into the presence of my commanding officer.

'Lieutenant Ogden, sir,' I said, 'C.O. of the *Lady Madeleine*, reporting for duty.' I then stood respectfully at attention with my cap under my arm. Captain D looked at me as if I were something the cat brought in. He then asked me very uncivilly what made me think I was suited to be a trawler captain, and what was my peace-time occupation. I was so unnerved by this welcome that I replied I had drifted into trawlers in 1940, and that my family were in the cigarette business. D eyed me scornfully, as if to let me know the Royal Navy had little use for shopkeepers. He then delivered his standing orders to new C.O.s with some further advice that if my ship and I did not come up to R.N. standards of seamanship, discipline and efficiency I could expect my stay on the Clyde to be a short one. He then dismissed me in the most peremptory manner. I had not felt so small and insignificant since my first day at Eton. As Oscar Wilde said, 'A gentleman never upsets anybody's feelings—unintentionally.'

I returned to *Lady M* in a state of the jitters. Nobody was more aware of my shortcomings as a C.O. than I was, but it was not I who had appointed myself to *Lady M*. It was 'Their Lordships' at the Admiralty.

I collected my officers and petty officers, the leading seamen and other key ratings, and told them that our ship was now attached to the 4th Clyde Escort Force. The insignia was a black-and-white check band round the funnel. I also told them that Captain D ashore looked like being a bore, so we had better use plenty of flannel in our dealings with him. The rest of the ships in our group consisted of a mixed bag of destroyers, corvettes and trawlers. Viscount Jocelyn was senior officer in *Achates*, David Magill Crighton had *Boreas* and 'Flash Alf' Turner—whose main claim to fame was his ability to deal with 'Two-ton Tessa', the barmaid at the Gourock Hotel—very aptly commanded H.M.S. *Boadicea*. The other ships were *Beagle, Bulldog, Beverly, Commandant Detroit, Heather, Lobelia, Primrose, Narcissus, Picotee, Ayrshire, Notts County, St. Apollo, King Sol, Daneman, Norwich City* and *St. Loman*. Sometimes some of the U.S.A. '10-knots-a-stack' destroyers used to start out with us if the weather was calm, but if it blew they had to return to harbour. I learned that we were to sail on our first convoy in three days' time.

Things started to hum in *Lady M*, as we were all determined we were not going to let the side down. We also got the ship's mail, which was always a fine tonic to everybody aboard. I had a letter from Sally, telling me her show was still running to packed houses in spite of the bombs and the black-out. She criticized me rather strongly for having addressed my last letter to her as Miss 'Solly' Carlton. I was just wondering how this could have happened— anything could happen at Belfast—when my eye fell on a parcel addressed to me in a familiar handwriting. I tore it open and found a beautiful white polo-necked sweater. I was overjoyed and amused to find that across the chest in dark blue a message had been knitted in. It read: 'Bears can't spell.' I unhooked the slipper from the lamp and put it under my pillow.

The bear sequence really went back to *The House at Pooh Corner* and contained many memories for Sally and me. Wol could spell 'Tuesday' and, like Pooh, I always found this most difficult, but it was agreed that:

> 'A bear however hard he tries,
> Gets tubby without exercise.'

Now I had been balancing myself on *Lady M*'s swaying decks, I had acquired a straddle that made me walk more like a bear than ever.

I went to the convoy conference at N.S.C.O. offices at Mary's Mount, where I saw for the first time the pattern of these quiet, sinister gatherings. The Commodore sat at the high table, flanked by the Naval Shipping Control Officer and the C.O. of the Escort. The grim-faced merchant captains and the C.O.s of the escort vessels formed the audience. Sailing orders and routing instructions were handed out (marked 'most secret') by N.S.C.O. and the Escort C.O. then told the room what had to be done in various emergencies. He adopted a rather cheerful note in his deliverance and intimated all would be well with convoy.

What he couldn't say was that he had no idea as to the perils of the voyage, and that apart from enemy aircraft, U-boats and a possible surface raider, the weather and collision risks were even worse enemies. He told the Commodore and the merchant captains that he would escort the convoy to 40 west. From there onwards there should be no dangers. Halifax, however, would still be more than a thousand miles away. The expressions on the faces of the merchant skippers remained dour and doubtful. They were brave men who knew they must follow their calling.

The conference then suddenly broke up and developed into a wild rush to get off.

Clutching my 'most secret' documents, I hastened back to *Lady M* to lock them up in my safe. As it turned out, I needn't have worried so much, for another C.O. had left the whole box of tricks in the local pub.

We were to sail at one minute past midnight. I spent a frenzied evening studying the convoy papers and the Western Approaches Convoy instructions. These consisted of what to do in various emergencies. They contained an elaborate R/T code, a series of completely impracticable instructions for illuminating the convoy with rockets and star shells (the worst possible thing to do) if were attacked at night. I put the papers and books back in the safe and went ashore with No.1 for dinner.

At 2330 I began to try to edge *Lady M* from the harbour wall. We were unfortunately the inside ship of three, and, although I had warned the C.O.s of the two outside ships I had to sail, when it came to letting me out into the stream these two ships were apparently deserted. To make matters worse, the night was black and slashed with driving rain.

At 0005 the base flashed, 'Why haven't you sailed on time?' I was too occupied to answer. If I had had the time I could have told Captain D and his staff a lot of things. As it was, I crept through the rain and darkness towards the boom ships moored opposite Dunoon. The blackout was so effective that I couldn't see the dimmed lights of the buoys or other vessels going seawards. The escort rendezvous was off the Mull of Kintyre at daybreak and I was seriously wondering if we should ever get there. A few minutes later a destroyer rushed by and called us up on the Aldis lamp. It turned out to be David Crighton, who signalled, 'What is your best speed?' I told him '13 knots.' He replied, 'Follow me,' and set off at about 20 knots. It was a nice thought, all the same.

Assembling a convoy with its escorts was quite a business. It took hours to organize and get everybody sorted out, and why the Germans never took more advantage of this I don't know, for the assembly points were common knowledge.

Our first duties with the 4th Clyde Escort Force took us halfway across the Atlantic and we soon settled down into the routine. Our position was on the port beam of the merchant ships, which were in a 'broad-front formation'. That is to say, in eight columns five ships deep. Alterations of course were made in the hours of darkness to deceive the enemy, which, although true in theory, often led to collisions and general confusion. The idea was that if a U-boat was about to attack the convoy, its commander would lose his firing angle.

In *Lady M* we spent the nights straining our eyes peering at the shadowy hulls of the merchantmen and hoping there would not be too many mysterious alterations of course—we still had no naval binoculars and relied on my ancient racing glasses, which had seen better days at Sandown Park.

Convoy HX123 (or whatever it was) reached 40 west 'without incident', which was really not surprising considering the Germans at this period had only a dozen active U-boats in the Atlantic, which is a big area to cover. And so it went on, anything up to thirty days at sea, a quick turn round and off again. Sometimes we ran into trouble, ships were lost by enemy action, but, by and large at that period, the 4th Clyde Escort Force and its charges were very fortunate. I was most glad of this, as in *Lady M* I soon discovered our failings as a fighting unit. The weather taxed our energies to the limit, largely because the ship was not equipped for the job we were doing. We could carry fresh meat for only five or six days, we had insufficient stowage for bread and vegetables, drinking water was rationed. The crew's mess decks were crowded and airless. We had no modern equipment, such as D/F, R.D.F or radar, and our W/T set was a very primitive affair. If we lost a convoy on a thick night the only chance of locating it was to go up into the crow's nest at daylight and look for its smoke. The smoke situation, one knew, was inevitable, so it always seemed so unnecessary to surround ourselves in secrecy when during the day the convoy was visible from some thirty miles away.

After we had been based at Greenock for six months a new Captain D arrived—Captain S.V. Jephson, who, being a seaman himself and just back for a rest from active fighting, was a very different type from his predecessor. 'Jeph' realized that the Atlantic escort trawlers were hopelessly under-equipped and set to work to put matters right. He came aboard *Lady M* and took a glass of gin in our wardroom. During the following year we got to know that he really cared about humble beings such as ourselves, with the result that we went out to show him we appreciated his friendship. Leadership is a strange, but unmistakable, quality. His foresight was just as well, for, later on, the shortage of destroyers was such that trawlers formed the escorts for the Icelandic convoys.

While we were in port I wrote some personal letters, and among them one to my friend George Sanders, who was in the U.S.A. George and I had both worked together in South America and had shared a flat together*. He had become a movie-actor and I was anxious to tell him of my affairs. I was somewhat surprised to receive the following:

---

* In 1960 George gave me a copy of his book entitled *The Memoirs of a Professional Cad*, and in it he describes some of the life we led together in Buenos Aires, but I thoroughly disagree with his version of these antics.

To: Lt. W.G. Ogden, R.N.V.R.   20th May 1941
                                              H.M.S. *Lady Madeleine*

P.C.114

POSTAL CENSORSHIP

Your letter to Hollywood, California, U.S.A.

By Admiralty instructions, a Member of the Naval Forces when writing to places outside the British Empire is not permitted to mention the name of his ship or establishment. Either of the following addresses may be used:

(a)   The address of a relative or friend in Great Britain or Northern Ireland, to whose care a reply can be sent for forwarding.

(b)   C/o Chief Postal Censor, London, with whom you must register your name and ship or Establishment. Letters are then forwarded to you without delay.

Note: Name of ship has been excised and letter sent on. Your name has been noted by the Postal Censor. It is not permitted to write to Enemy or Enemy Occupied Territory, except through the British Red Cross or Messrs. Thomas Cook and Son.

This raised the interesting problem of whether in the eyes of the authorities California came in the category of Enemy or Enemy Occupied Territory.

On one convoy, after the first day, it was discovered that three ships had sailed in error. The S.O. of the escort detailed *Lady M* and *Ayrshire* to escort them back to port. The ships were detached and formed up in line ahead with the trawler on either bow of the leading ship, *Ayrshire* to port, *Lady M* to starboard. We were the senior ship. As the light began to fade, I went back to signal the last ship, which was straggling behind to close up. He took no notice, so I went closer and yelled at him through my megaphone. After about half an hour we caught up with the leading ships. As I was going to my night station on the beam, the leading ship swung sharply off to starboard. I sheered off too, thinking he had seen a mine. He had, in point of fact, nearly run into a U-boat on the surface. If he had held his course he could probably have rammed it. As he swung off, he flashed a signal-lamp wildly and blew the ship's siren. The second ship held her course and so did the straggler. I increased speed, rang the alarm gongs for A/S stations and called *Ayrshire* on the R/T to ask if they had seen anything. They hadn't. I was trying to signal to the leading ship to find out why he had suddenly altered course when there was a muffled thud, an orange sheet of flame, followed by a shower of red sparks as torpedoes hit the last ship on her port side. This was the first time I had been really close to a torpedoing. We were less than half a cable away on the starboard hand. I headed *Lady M* towards the explosion and signalled *Ayrshire* to take care of the two ships ahead. When I came to where the ship had been there was a very strong smell of cordite, a pool of oil, some wreckage, but that was all. No boats—no survivors.

It was now dark, and a squall had suddenly blown up. Were there any survivors, I wondered, and was the U-boat waiting on the surface to put a 'fish' into us? I fired off two magnesium rockets, but saw nothing. I then went off in the direction from which the torpedoes had come, searching for the U-boat with the asdic set. We searched the area in vain, so I ordered the 4 in.-gun crew to fire six rounds of star shell. I wanted to see if any lifeboats were distinguishable, or if the U-boat was still on the surface. After we had fired two star shells a gun was fired at close range in our direction. I ordered our gun crew to load with H.E. and fire in the direction of the flash. Just at that second we made out the shape of *Ayrshire*, so held our fire. It afterwards turned out that she had come back thinking we were being attacked, and the flash we saw was a star shell she had fired, which hadn't exploded. With a star shell you must use a half-charge, and in the dark it's difficult to tell which is which. A near go, all the same. *Lady M* continued to search the area and *Ayrshire* went off after the other ships. We made one or two depth-charge attacks, more with the idea of letting a U-boat know we were on the job than from any established asdic contact. Later we set course for the other ships. When we were within sight of the Butt of Lewis lighthouse our hydrophones produced ominous sounds. I could hear electric motors running, mechanical clankings and a tick, tick, tick. The sounds were faint but distinct, and I judged they came from a U-boat sitting on the bottom. We got a firm asdic 'contact', but it didn't move. By the chart we were in about 50 fathoms. Setting the depth-charges to go off at 300 ft. we dropped them over the target. To my horror and astonishment, the whole lot went off as soon as they touched the water, shaking *Lady M* from stem to stern. I cursed the officer whose duty it was to see the D/C were correctly set, and sent the first lieutenant to go and set another pattern at maximum depth. We tried again with similar results. This time the chief rushed up to the bridge and said if I dropped any more charges which went off at 'no feet' I should sink the ship, so we hung about looking for survivors.

At daylight we found a fishing trawler had picked up a boatload, including the captain, who told me that his ship had gone down in two minutes. He had seen me looking for him, but was too scared to shout or show a light, as he thought the U-boat might machine-gun him.

I went back to base, not feeling at all pleased with myself or *Lady M*. I tried to find out what was the matter with my depth-charges, but never succeeded. The A/S authorities gave me an entirely new consignment of a different design, which later on proved satisfactory.

The following is the official description of this incident:

SECRET

U-BOAT ATTACK ON S.S. INGER
ON 23rd AUGUST, 1941

From: THE CAPTAIN (D) GREENOCK, ALBERT HARBOUR, GREENOCK

Date: 8th September, 1941   No. 6059/64

To: THE COMMANDER-IN-CHIEF, WESTERN APPROACHES

Copies to:
The Director of A/S Warfare, Admiralty
The Captain (D) Liverpool
The Captain (D) Londonderry

The Senior Officer, 4th Escort Group
The Commanding Officer, H.M.T. *Lady Madeleine*
The Commanding Officer, H.M.T. *Ayrshire*

The following report is forwarded. All times are British Summer time.

1.   At 2210 on 23rd August, 1941, H.M. Trawlers *Lady Madeleine* (Senior Officer) and *Ayrshire* were in approximate position 585°8′N, 7°50′W escorting three ships to Loch Ewe. The convoy was in line ahead in the order *British Colony, President Francqui* and *Inger*, steering 115° at 8 knots. The first two ships were tankers.

2.   *Lady Madeleine* and *Ayrshire* were on the starboard and port bow respectively.

3.   The light was poor being between dusk and dark. Sea and swell 30—wind force 5 from NNW.

4.   Prior to taking up escorting positions on the quarters of the convoy for the night, *Lady Madeleine* dropped back to chase up *Inger* who was astern of station, being about 5 cables astern of *President Francqui*.

5.   At 2250/23 ss. *British Colony* sighted a U-boat close under her port bow. She immediately sounded two groups of 5 blasts on her siren, altered course to starboard and made a signal by light to *Lady Madeleine*.

6.   The U-boat was also seen by *President Francqui* but this ship appears to have made no signal and taken no action.

7.   At 2252/23 ss. *Inger* who was by this time in station, and who had heard *British Colony*'s siren but had seen nothing, was struck by a torpedo on her port side in the boiler room. A second torpedo struck No. 4 hatch as she turned over, and the vessel sank in two minutes.

8.   H.M.T. *Lady Madeleine* was close on the starboard bow of *President Francqui* when the leading ship altered to starboard. She had heard the siren and was endeavouring to read a signal by light from *British Colony*, when she saw the heard *Inger* torpedoed.

9.   After asking *Ayrshire* by R/T if she had seen what happened, *Lady Madeleine* proceeded to the position where *Inger* had sunk and searched the area. A rain squall had come down and the visibility was down to 1000 yards. No asdic contact was obtained. *Ayrshire* was ordered to proceed with the two tankers to Loch Ewe and *Lady Madeleine* continued to search firing snowflake rockets and starshell.

10.   *Ayrshire* was about 1500 yards on the port bow of *British Colony* when she heard the siren at 2250/23. She immediately turned towards the convoy and two small explosions were heard and a flash seen apparently in the direction of *Inger*.

11.   *Ayrshire* then proceeded after the convoy as ordered until 2300/23 when snowflake rockets were sighted. These were being fired by *Lady Madeleine*. *Ayrshire* turned about and fired starshell in the direction of the rockets, then proceeded with the convoy.

12.   At 0030/24 when abreast the starboard beam of the tankers *Ayrshire* detected strong hydrophone effect, and shortly afterwards echo contact was obtained. An attack was delivered with 5 charges set to 250 feet and the last charge to 150 feet. Contact was not regained and there was no visible result of the attack.

S. V. JEPHSON

CAPTAIN

Enclosures:
Copy of Report of Commanding Officer, H.M.T. *Lady Madeleine*
Copy of Report of Commanding Officer, H.M.T. *Ayrshire*
Report of Attack on Enemy Submarine
Track Chart
Recorder Trace—Commander-in-Chief, Western Approaches only.
To Commander-in-Chief, Western Approaches & D A/S W. Only.

T o return to the human side of things, I had now got to know my crew, and what's more they had got to know me. We had our differences, which were taken in good heart by both sides, but I had a problem with Donald.

This pleasant lowland Scot always wore a cloth cap the wrong way round and so we called him 'Speedy'. As soon as we were alongside, he would disappear, and be helped aboard, completely plastered, just before we sailed. I tried everything to break him of this habit, but one day he missed the ship and got himself put into the brig with a label of 'ninety days cells' round his neck. Two months afterwards, when we were in port, he reappeared with his usual slow smile and informed me he had come to rejoin the ship.

'How did you get out of the brig?' I said.

'They wouldn't keep me any longer, sir,' he replied.

'What was it like?' I asked him.

'Well, it was all right, sir; the food was much better than in the ship, and there wasn't much work to do.'

'It's all very well for you, Donald,' I said, 'coming back to the ship and telling me what a good time you had in prison, but I had to sail without you and was short of a quartermaster. I don't mind telling you I'm fed up with your drunken ways.'

Suddenly the smile fled from Donald's freckled face and was replaced by a look of pain. 'It wasn't the drink, sir, you know, I could nay do that to you.'

'Well, you missed the ship, didn't you? What did happen?' I asked him.

'It was on account of the kid, sir.'

'What kid, Donald? As far as your papers are concerned, you come from Aberdeen and are not married.'

'It was in that last air-raid, sir, his mother got killed.'

'You mean it was your kid? How old is it?'

Donald's frank blue eyes were clouded. 'He's about that high,' he said, measuring off about two feet from the deck. 'You see, sir, I had to get him fixed up in another home and it wasn't easy.' We were both now thoroughly embarrassed. I poured out two half-tumblers of whisky and handed him one.

'I'm sorry, Donald,' I said. 'Here's luck to the young 'un and you can rejoin the ship.'

Donald gave me a look I shall never forget. All he said was, 'You'll nay regret it,' as he downed his whisky and then shambled out of my cabin.

As it turned out, Donald, by his touch on the steering wheel, was to save our lives again and again. Born to the sea, he could steer *Lady M* round a sixpence.

This story has a sequel, which I hope Donald never gets to know about. While thinking over the compassionate circumstances of Donald's troubles, I came to the conclusion that the Maintenance Captain should not have sentenced one of my crew without first consulting me. I also discovered that this man's only claim to glory was that in 1940 he had run a patrol boat ashore at Cape Town. I decided to call upon him. The interview went wrong from the word 'go'.

Before I had got started this stuffy old man informed me that I had no right to be a commanding officer, that I had no conception of how to run my ship according to K.R. and A.I. and that he wasn't interested in any 'compassionate circumstances' I put forward on Donald's behalf.

This unprovoked attack on myself and *Lady M* annoyed me, so I said, 'I can quite understand that, as I understand you are interested in running H.M. ships ashore in faraway places.' I've seldom seen a man boil over so fast. He struck a bell on his desk and a sentry approached. He summoned his master-at-arms and before I knew what was going on I found I was under arrest. Jeph got me out of it and sent the ship in a great hurry off to Campbeltown. He tore a strip off me all the same. However, when we got back from our next convoy I found I had been 'mentioned in dispatches' and the Maintenance Captain had gone elsewhere.

I notice that on 7th August 1941 I wrote the following letter to Captain D which shows the difficulties we were up against:

To: Capt. D. Greenock.

From: C.O. *Lady Madeleine*   Date: 7.8.41

Sir,

With regard to your 1333/5 I would like to bring certain facts to your notice which may not be appreciated and which to me are very real problems; I would in fact ask your help in this matter—

1. The personnel allotted to this type of ship is very unsatisfactory. The type of man we get from Lowestoft has had little or no training and being H/O may be anybody from a bricklayer to a bank clerk. There is nobody in this ship who has had any experience of R.N. ships, or R.N. matters. There are no petty officers in this ship and the Coxswain is a leading seaman. The engine room

staff consists of two engine men and four stokers. The 2nd being an older hand than the acting Chief. We do not carry an H.S.D. so cannot cope with serious asdic repairs at sea.

My No.1 is ashore with pneumonia and my No.2 has been given another appointment. I am therefore left with my No.3, a R.N.V.R. sub and a new R.N.V.R. sub who is quite unfitted for this type of ship, and has never been to sea before as an officer. I have also borrowed a midshipman for the time being. This means I have to do most of the watch keeping myself, and almost everything else as well.

2. When these ships were converted it was thought they would carry a complement of about 20 to 25 hands and 3 officers. I now have a complement of 37 and the congestion does not make for efficiency. Should you visit the ship I think you would agree.

3. I have from time to time applied for more A.A. guns but nothing has happened. The present situation is one .5 aft and 2 single Lewis guns on the veranda wings. There is however no V/P from the aft gun to the bridge.

4. For the past year, on average our escort duties have taken us to sea for periods of 12 days at a time. Our meat lasts for 6 to 7 days and bread about the same. Fresh water forward lasts for about 5 days.

5. We have no medical supplies and do not carry a sick bay attendant.

6. We have only one efficient pair of A/S head-phones.

7. We have only two D/C Throwers whereas there is no reason at all why we should not carry 4 which would enable us to fire a 10 charge pattern.

8. In the past, ships in various Escort groups have been manned and equipped according to their own classification which results in some ships getting everything and others practically nothing. As we all do the same work it is suggested that the requirements of the Group be considered rather than individual ships. We, for instance, need a lot of gear to bring us up to our full

efficiency which is at present denied to us because we are only a 'Trawler'.

I have the honour to be, Sir,
Your obedient Servant,
GRAEME OGDEN
Lt. R.N.V.R.

Captain S.V. Jephson was a man after my own heart, and did in the end get his trawlers fully equipped as fighting ships. In our case we had to wait until we had a major refit at Ardrossan in March 1942 prior to going to Russia, but it was he who made this possible.

In September, for no apparent reason, Brian Westwood got pneumonia, and so I was without a first lieutenant, until one fine day Geoffrey Angus arrived. David Lynx Odham left us to become a gunnery expert, and 'McTavish', whose correct name is McAlistair Weir, relieved him. But before we say goodbye to David we must go back to one very foggy day when, homeward bound, I was trying to make a landfall on the Butt of Lewis. I thought we were too far to the south'ard but had 'run the distance', so was hoping to see something soon. We didn't really know where we were, so on sighting a fishing trawler we closed her and asked for some advice.

Fishermen usually know where they are, because they rely on the bottom of the ocean and the banks on which they fish. I told David, who was on watch, to get the loud-hailer going and ask for a course to the Butt of Lewis. A very Winchester voice went floating over the waves—'I say, trawlah, can you direct me to the...ah...the Butt of Lewis?' The skipper of the fishing trawler failed to interpret this sort of language, but by this time our lads were yelling at him in all too familiar language. He gave us a course which took us round the Butt, although we never saw its light in the swirling wet fog.

When David left us Bill became No.2 and Weir took over as No.3. This turned out to be the team which were to stay and fight together until 1943. We also changed coxswains. When Turner arrived I was a little dubious, as he was a pocket-sized individual with a weather-beaten face and a marked sense of humour. As it turned out, he was a godsend to me and *Lady M*. He was an ex-R.N. type, who knew all about the Royal Navy. He had, in fact, served several commissions in the *Royal Sovereign*, and had been in charge of its unique steam laundry, the pride of which had been the shirt-and-collar machine. This infernal contraption had nearly ended Turner's life, for, caught with his trousers down by an admiral's inspection, he had been obliged to dive into an immense copper to avoid being observed. From the inside of this fastness he heard his commanding officer ask the visiting admiral if he would like to see 'the wheels go round', referring to the series of large metal fins revolving in the copper. Fortunately the admiral declined this invitation, and Turner was spared to me. He was a nippy little man, who might well once have been aloft in the upper royals of a barque.

He was a tremendous asset at sing-songs, for he would appear wearing a battered old top-hat and a monocle, then, having taken out his teeth, he would sing, 'I Stuttered too Much'. This turn was a great success wherever we happened to be.

Quite apart from anything else, without any help from Turner *Lady M* was a musically minded ship. While we were in Belfast some thoughtful religious society had presented *Lady M* with an organ. I had managed to swop this for a piano, and, what's more, arrange for Geordie to join the ship as assistant cook. Geordie had earned his peacetime living as pianist in a jazz band. We also had a first-class guitarist in Stoker Gaunt, plus Glue (the A.A. gunner), with his home-made drums. I think we must have been the original skiffle group. Our repertoire consisted of such songs as 'My Brother Sylvest', 'Old McDonald had a Farm', 'Round the Marble Arch', 'Out in the Cold, Cold Snow', 'Goodnight, Sweetheart' and 'Old Shanty Town'. There was another side to the ship's musical activities too. While at Londonderry I had bought a record, the 'Bridge of Athlone', a stirring Irish jig which I adopted as a sailing tune. The rhythm corresponded to the beat of the ship's propeller and replaced an official ship's band when we left harbour.

Sally sent me a record called 'Off she goes in the North', which was a Scottish reel, and in her honour I used to play this over the ship's loud-hailer system when we were picking up survivors from sinking ships. Many of the exhausted sailors we rescued from the drink told me afterwards that the music gave them hope, and courage to hold on a little longer, until we could get them aboard *Lady Madeleine*.

Besides the Scottish reel, Sally had sent me another record. On one side the vocalist told me about 'The blind man on the corner who sings the Beale Street Blues', and on the other side Bessie Smith sang this to me:

> 'Love, oh love, oh careless love,
> You fly right to my head like wine,
> You've wrecked the heart of many a gal,
> And you nearly wrecked this life of mine.'

Living as I was, surrounded by naval codes and top secret ciphers, I had got myself into the frame of mind of trying to decode even the simplest matters. Now I wondered if this record contained a hidden message. Was I supposed to be the blind man on the corner and guilty of careless love?

That night I had a record dream. I dreamed that I was sailing a yacht through the purple waters of some idyllic sea. Suddenly a squall struck. Spurting rain drenched the thrashing sails, for seconds the yacht shuddered, then capsized, throwing me into the sea. When the squall had passed I drifted idly with a warm current, which carried me into sunlit waters, flecked with golden lights outlined by dark-green shadows. Soon a tropical island came in sight surrounded by swaying palm trees. I swam lazily to the shore and was greeted by a castaway dressed in rags.

'Who are you?' I asked.

'I'm the blind man on the corner,' the stranger replied. I brushed past this apparition with his dead, staring eyes and plunged into the jungle. I knew I was searching for Sally and, as I pressed deep into the fern-clad dell, the red tropical flowers resembled her hair and the rustle of the trade wind in the coconut palms above sounded like her humming the melody of 'Careless Love'. I heard a bell ring. Faintly at first and then so strongly I knew it for what it was. The watch was changing aboard *Lady M.*

I wrote to Sally to thank her for the records and also told her about my dream. In her next letter she said she was delighted about the reel being played at sea during rescue operations. Her only comment about my dream was that if, like a good seaman, I had looked to see if my barometer was rising or falling the whole incident could have been avoided. Oh! Well...there goes romance. Thank goodness my other Sea Lady can't write—let alone spell.

Just prior to the 'Turneresque' period I made a serious error which, I am sure, he with his knowledge of R.N. technique would have stopped me doing. While in port, I received a signal from the depot ship, H.M.S. *Hecla*, to the effect that a ten-day training course was offered to ships' cooks. As our official cook, Ricketts, was an ex-garage hand from Birmingham, who no doubt was an excellent chap to change the oil in one's car or grind in the valves, I thought this was a good thing, so sent him off to *Hecla* and relied on Geordie to cook at sea. On returning to Greenock after our next convoy, he rejoined the ship and reported to me. I told him we wanted a special dinner that night and suggested we started with Sole Colbert or Lobster Cardinal. Which could he do best?

'Do you know, sir,' spluttered Ricketts, 'I've kept a note of what I had to do each day and I never did any cooking at all.'

'That's a fine story,' I said. 'What the dickens did you do?'

'I scrubbed the decks, cleaned and blacked the stoves and peeled the potatoes.'

In a rage, I sent for the signalman and made a signal in this sense—'To C.O. H.M.S. *Hecla*—from C.O. *Lady Madeleine*. I sent my cook for instruction in cooking, not in scrubbing the deck and cleaning stoves. Full report follows.' Dismissing the matter from my mind, I went down to lunch. Early in the afternoon things began to happen, which ended up by my going off in the captain of the *Hecla*'s motor boat, to report to him in his ship. The *Hecla* was a 20,000-ton depot repair ship and on going on board I was greeted by the O.O.W., who took me off the C.O., who, in a fury, was stamping about his quarter deck. The lenses were rattling in his telescope.

'Are you the C.O. of the *Lady Madeleine*?' he barked.

'Yes, sir.'

'What's your name and rank?'

'Lieutenant Ogden, sir...R.N.V.R.' I added hastily.

'Well, Lieutenant Ogden, R.N.R.V., I may as well tell you you made to me, a Captain R.N., a very rude signal.'

I didn't speak, it's much safer not to on these occasions.

'What do you mean by such impertinence? Who do you think you are, sending me signals like that? Are you seriously suggesting that this...cook of yours didn't receive proper instruction?'

'Yes, sir,' I ventured.

'Do you really mean...? Come down to my cabin.'

We descended. I offed cap and stood in what I thought was a respectful attitude. The cabin was full of flowers, and I felt slightly better.

'Don't stand like that,' said Captain Coltart. 'Sit down. Have a cigarette. Tea, whisky-and-soda?'

He pressed a bell—the spell was broken. Together we established the facts, which were more or less as I had stated. Nobody could have been more charming, and I much regretted making such a tactless signal.

Talking of signals, wise or unwise, Leo Gradwell made some good ones. When he got leave to be with his wife when his son was due to arrive, the lad was late in putting in an appearance. So Leo wired to D: 'Request extension leave—E.T.A. delayed' (E.T.A. being the usual abbreviation used for estimated time of arrival when telling your base when to expect you). I forgot what D replied, but when Master Gradwell turned up Leo wired: 'Red-and-white buoy adrift from moorings—am returning to base.'

On our next Atlantic convoy we had fair weather and a full moon. The escort force was a small one, and our position was on the port bow of the convoy. All went smoothly and the days and nights slipped quickly by as we sailed beneath towering Atlantic skies and vivid stars.

One night I had a premonition that something was going to happen, so I warned the duty watch, the chief and my officers that I thought we were in for some excitement. It was an ideal night for a U-boat attack, there being enough sea running to make it difficult to see a periscope feather or a submarine silhouette outside the path of the moon. These were the conditions a U-boat likes, because travelling fast on the surface, the captain could take up his position ahead of the convoy. His instruments told him its speed and course and when to fire his torpedoes. He then dived (very often under the convoy) and made his getaway, for the escorts could not locate it on their asdics on account of the noise made by the ships' propellers. A U-boat would normally not crash-dive under helm, but once it had done so it had a turning circle of about 400 yds. and could do 7½ knots under water.

On this particular night we hadn't long to wait. Geoff took over as asdic C.O. and about an hour later the operator reported a 'slight hydrophone effect 2,500 yds., Red 80'.

'Here we go,' I said to Geoff, and pointed the ship towards the contact. Geoff put on his headphones and listened.

'Sounds good,' he said. 'Want to listen?' I put on the phones and heard the thud of diesel motors which could only mean a U-boat on the surface. I took up my night glasses and scanned the dark sea. At that moment the starboard look-out, a fisherman called

Armstrong, started yelling and pointing. My heart jumped into my mouth as I rang the alarm gong. A U-boat, well trimmed down, was crossing our bows, from port to starboard.

I think she had seen us and was actually diving, because half her conning tower was submerged. We were doing about 12 knots at the time, so all we could do was to try and ram by going hard a-starboard. Twelve knots is about 400 yds. a minute, and turning to lay off the U-boat's course, I reckoned we had about 200 yds. to go if we were going to succeed. The next thirty seconds seemed like eternity as we waited for the crunch. There was no crunch, but we went near enough to upset the U-boat's trim and we saw her break surface to starboard and then disappear again. Soon we got a strong asdic contact and held on to it while we steamed off to get into position to make our attacking run in. Depth-charges were set shallow. In we came at full speed. The charges exploded, throwing up mountains of silver water in the moonlight, and I heard the aft party give a cheer. The .5 machine gun also opened fire with a staccato rattle.

Our depth-charges had surfaced the U-boat, but we only caught a fleeting glimpse of it. I turned *Lady M* away to come in for another attack. Getting into position to attack is a bad moment, as it is then one can lose contact with the enemy. In this attack our asdic operator held on and at last the ship was again in an attacking position. I told the chief to 'give her the gun' and *Lady M* raced towards the target, but before we were near enough to drop our depth-charges our for'ard gun started firing—Mac had previous orders from me to fire as soon as he saw the enemy. This time I had a good view of the U-boat, which was again bobbing about on the surface, and again we tried to ram. We were too much to port to get on to a ramming course, but I turned towards it. The U-boat slithered down *Lady M*'s side. I could have hit it with a cricket ball. The machine-gunners sprayed the U-boat but with little or no effect. When I judged our stern was as near the German as we could get I pressed the D/C firing bells. There was the most unholy explosion, *Lady M* shook like a leaf and Geoff and I clung on to the A/S bridge. The ship's electric current failed. We were in complete darkness, with no instruments functioning. We both ran out on to the bridge sponson to see if we had scored a hit. The aft party were cheering, but I did not see the U-boat sink, as most of the crew imagined they had. In the excitement I had forgotten to stop the ship, which was still speeding away from the scene of our last attack. By the time I had stopped her I hadn't any idea of where we had last attacked the U-boat, as the compass light had gone out and the flare we had dropped to mark the spot had got blown to bits. By this time two destroyers had arrived on the scene and proceeded to search the area. I had lost my own bearings and given ourselves and the ship such a shaking that we were not much help to anybody. Later we rigged some auxiliary lighting and joined in a star-shell search, but nothing further was seen. The escort being small, the S.O. called off the search and we all rejoined the convoy. Whatever else may have happened, I am convinced that the U-boat was coming in to attack the convoy and we caught him in the act. The aggravating thought is that I shall never know if we sunk this U-boat or only winged it. Whatever the result may have been, I would not have cared to have been aboard U-whatever it was that particular evening.

We got back to Greenock on Thursday after this convoy, and prayed that we would have a few days in port. The ship's mail was delivered and, to my great joy, there was a letter from Sally. My heart sang, for it appeared there was a chance of her getting to Glasgow for the week-end, her show having gone on tour and being due to reopen at Manchester on the Monday. She could, I read, arrive in Glasgow at noon that Saturday. Would I send a telegram if this was all right and meet her at Glasgow Central station at noon? I dashed ashore and cabled: 'Yes, wonderful.' The thought of seeing Sally, with her shoulder-long red hair and her sea-blue eyes, thrilled me to such an extent I hardly knew what I was doing for the next twenty-four hours. I spent the time making the most exciting plans as to what we should do, and what chances there might be of introducing her to my other love—*Lady Madeleine*.

At 0900 on Saturday my signalman knocked on my cabin door and gave me the day's signals. To my horror, I saw a pink signal from the base, ordering *Lady M* to coal at the coal-tip off Gourock at 1100 that day. Bombs, torpedoes, Atlantic gales I could face with equilibrium, but a disappointment of this sort was more than I could bear. My dreams were to be smothered in coal-dust. I leapt up from my desk in a fury, took a tumbler, filled it with whisky and drank it off at a gulp. As if my magic, Squires suddenly appeared. The fact of his seeing me throwing Scotch down my throat so early in the morning steadied me. It also gave me an idea which I acted on at once.

'Squires' I said, 'I need your assistance.

Squires looked at the whisky bottle.

'Very good,' I said. 'Help yourself.'

'Now, look here,' I continued, 'I am in a most infuriating and difficult position. My...er...friend Miss Carlton is arriving at Glasgow Central Station at 1200 today, and I was going to meet her, but I have just received a signal from the base ordering the ship to leave immediately for Gourock to coal. It is imperative that somebody meets Miss Carlton and as I can't—you must.'

'Exactly, sire,' Squires answered, finishing his drink and looking towards the bottle rack.

'Right, then, you change immediately into your No.1s and proceed to Glasgow forthwith. You can't mistake Miss Carlton, she has red hair and—'

'I have observed Miss Carlton on the stage,' Squires announced.

'Very good. Now, you will need some money.' I unlocked the ship's safe, where I always kept several pounds in cash of my own money, and gave Squires a few notes.

'Your orders are,' I said sternly, 'to meet Miss Carlton, arrange hotel accommodation for her and explain why I can't be present. You are to render her any service you can...but I don't mean...'

Squires held up his hands, as if to reproach me for having such shocking ideas.

'Then you are to leave a note with the barman at the Central Hotel as to what arrangements you have made, and tell Miss Carlton that I will get to Glasgow with the speed of light, once I have coaled this something ship.'

'I understand perfectly,' Squires said, giving me one of his sly looks and refilling his glass.

'On your way,' I commanded; 'and if you let me down I'll murder you.'

Squires made one of his stiff bows, saluted and disappeared.

I mustered the crew aft and told them the bad news. I knew they wanted to go ashore just as badly as I did, so I impressed on them that the harder we all worked the sooner we should be free. We sailed in record time and got down to the filthy business of coaling ship as if our lives depended on it. By 1800 we were back at Greenock and the liberty-men went ashore. I tried to get the grime off myself, but such was my hurry I wasn't very successful. I stuffed some money into my pocket and hastily made a parcel of all the presents I had bought for Sally from Iceland, where one could get American stockings, lipsticks, perfume and pretties. This I put into a black, official Admiralty briefcase. I put my own overnight things, as usual, into my gasmask case and left a note for No.1 telling him not to expect me until Sunday morning.

Once ashore, I headed for D's office. I thought it unlikely he or any of his staff would be about at 1830 on a Saturday evening. On arrival I found a Wren who told me the Admiral was throwing a cocktail party and everybody was there. She looked at me with some alarm, and on catching sight of myself in a mirror I was not surprised—I looked like a chimney-sweep.

'I just popped in to have a word with the duty officer,' I told her.

'He's gone out for a few minutes,' she replied.

'I'll go into his room and wait for him.' Once there, I seized the red telephone, which was a direct line to F.O.I.C.'s offices in

Glasgow, and asked for the duty officer. When he came through I briskly enquired when *Lady M* was due to sail. I could hear him shuffling some papers about, and after what seemed like an age he told me we were to sail with Convoy S.C. 321 on Wednesday. I put the receiver down and beat it, passing the duty officer on my way out. I then hurried round to Naval Transport. Here I was greeted by a tired and bored C.P.O., who informed me that all cars had gone to the Admiral's party. I told him I wanted transport to Glasgow *toute suite*. It was dark in the garage and I kept my grimy face well out of sight.

'You're out of luck, chum,' was all he said. True enough, there wasn't a car or a driver in sight, but there was a motor-bike leaning against the wall. I was getting desperate. Six valuable hours had slipped by which I might have spent with Sally.

'Who does the bike belong to?' I asked him.

'Me.'

'Like to hire it to me?' I said quickly, at the same time offering him a ten-shilling note.

I reached Glasgow in about half an hour and made for the bar at the Central Hotel. There, I need hardly say, I found Squires in a state of intoxication. On my appearance, he staggered to his feet, saluted and then lost his balance and subsided on to a sofa. I don't know what I said to him, but whatever it was it didn't take the drunken smile off his face. Without speaking, he handed me a piece of paper with an address on it—somewhere in Bearsden. Below was written: 'Mission complete—Respectfully Alfred Squires.'

Unfortunately the bar was full of people and we were attracting a certain amount of attention, otherwise I would have brought Squires to his senses with a left hook. As it was, I managed to extract most of the money I had given him, and make him understand that if he didn't go back to the ship I would have him arrested for drunkenness. I gave the barman a quid and told him not to give Squires any more to drink. In a state of nervous confusion I left the hotel and took a taxi to Bearsden. This Glasgow suburb is what house agents would call 'a good residential area' and why on earth Squires had brought Sally here I couldn't imagine. I knew the Glasgow hotels were often full up at week-ends, but why Bearsden of all places? A boarding house owned by his aunt? The taxi stopped before a superior-looking residence. I checked the address in the blackout, paid off the cab, and went up the steps two at a time.

R ailway stations in wartime are gloomy impersonal places, yet filled with high tragedy. Men en route for ships from which they may never return, last-minute embraces from sweethearts and wives, half-demented mothers searching for their children and above all the violent hiss of escaping steam and the clanking of aged engines.

I said goodbye to Sally at the Midland Station and, although every tick of the clock took her farther away from me, I couldn't leave the platform. All the love and laughter of the last few hours was evaporating into the stinking station air.

Slowly, I made my way back to Greenock in a halting train, and every time it stopped I was tempted to get out and make for Manchester. I had completely forgotten about the motor-bike—this turned out to be rather an expensive omission.

I went abroad *Lady M* with a sense of guilt, for, having granted myself twenty-four hours' leave, without telling my superiors, I wasn't quite sure what I was going to say if anything had gone wrong with the ship in my absence. When I reached my cabin I was surprised to see Squires, whom until then I had forgotten about. He was busy fussing over a bowl of red roses on my chart table. I threw my gasmask case on my bunk and regarded him with amazement.

'Good evening, sire,' he said, without blinking an eyelid, 'I was just arranging some flowers Miss Carlton asked me to get for you.'

I felt the blood surge back into my veins. 'Thanks, Squires,' I said. 'That will be all for this evening.'

A gentleman's gentleman, I thought, is a great asset even in the middle of a war.

I t was now nearing the end of May, and we sailed away to Iceland
on the following Wednesday 'as anticipated'. If there's one place
I hate more than another it's Iceland. Even the Danes can't stand
it. They have a word for its inhabitants, which means 'cod-fish-
with-boots-on.' These islanders are sly and grasping. As far as we
were concerned, the only benefit of going ashore at Reykjavik was
that one could buy all sorts of things which had become unavailable at home. I could start a new shopping chest for Sally.

Almost the whole country is composed of glaciers and volcanic
rocks, and is a miserable, desolate wilderness. In 1939 the country
was bankrupt. Now it is more like a Canadian mining town.
'Recky' itself looks like a Scandinavian town surrounded by acres
of Nissen huts. When the British occupied the place, in order to
get there before the Germans, in April 1940, I understand it was a
pretty good pantomime. One story goes that after the marines had
gone ashore the next party consisted of Eskimo-speaking inter-
preters and the railway transport officers. As the Icelanders speak
a sort of Danish patois, the former were a little out of their depth,

and when the top brass of the R.T.O. demanded to be taken to the railway station they were surprised to learn that there is not one yard of railway track in Iceland.

A railway warrant printed in English from Reykjavik to Seydisfjörd must be quite a curiosity. Anyhow, we were bound for Iceland whether we liked it or not.

After we had been at sea for two days Haliday, the senior W/T operator, sent a message to the bridge asking if he could see me in private.

I saw Haliday in my cabin, thinking that our primitive wireless set had packed up and that we were 'off the ether', but he had very different news. He was, I should tell you, a particularly intelligent young man and most knowledgeable about radio, radar and electronics. He had, he said, rigged up some experimental Radio Directional Finding apparatus of his own design. In a great state of excitement he explained to me that by using this home-made outfit in conjunction with the ship's W/T set he had detected a sudden increase in naval W/T activity. The signals were of the highest priority (Urgent—break—Operational) and in Naval Cipher A. We could not decipher these signals, but Haliday claimed to have established that they originated from somewhere in the Denmark Strait. This, he suggested, might mean that a German surface raider was about. I thanked Haliday for his keen interest and ordered him to continue to listen in and keep me informed how things were going, but on no account to mention his ideas to anybody else in the ship. I made a note in the ship's log; the day was 23rd May.

The weather being fine, I went back on to the bridge and took some sun-sights, then returned to my cabin to work them out and check our position on the chart. While I was doing this I began to feel rather queasy. We were a small, slow convoy of four trawlers, escorting fourteen merchant ships, and, should 'Sparks' be correct, it was on the cards that the worst fate of all might be in store for us.

The problem of a German battle squadron at sea, intent on annihilating our convoys, filled my mind, for things were quite bad enough with the losses inflicted by aircraft and U-boats. I knew that, a month before, the eastward-bound convoy S.C. 26 had lost a dozen ships to U-boats in one night and also that the Germans were boasting that their two top-scoring U-boat aces—Prien and Kretschmer—had between them accounted for half a million tons of our shipping. During the first four months of 1941 over 150 ships had been torpedoed. The picture looked grim, but one always felt that there was some escape from U-boat and aircraft attacks, if only on the assumption that the attackers carried a limited number of bombs and torpedoes. The terrifying thought of a chance encounter with a German battle squadron meant a massacre from which there would be no hope of escape.

Having decided as accurately as I could where we were from my observed and estimated positions, I charted the possible course of German surface raiders breaking into the Atlantic via the Denmark Strait. Our HX (Halifax) convoys were usually routed between 55°N and 60°N, depending on the position of the ice edge. When the ice breaks up in the spring and forms into bergs the southern course was used. A raider would presumably head for about 40°W and 55°N, then make a wide southerly sweep towards the French Atlantic ports such as St. Nazaire. On the face of it, it seemed unlikely that we should come into contact with any such enemy force, and the whole thing was a supposition, anyway. What seemed more likely was that we might see a British battle fleet steaming westwards from Scapa Flow.

Although the weather was fine, there were thick patches of fog about and I became very nervous as to what I should do if a battleship at high speed suddenly loomed out of the fog.

We had not received any official signals as to a German raider being at sea. 'The book' said that on sighting an enemy force an escort should immediately make an enemy-sighting report, giving position, course and speed, then lay a smoke-screen round the convoy. Supposing I mistook our battleships for the German and made the requisite signal to Admiralty in the simple code we carried? The Germans would obviously read the code and then know the position of our advancing fleet. On the other hand, if I sighted a German battle cruiser and failed to report it I would have committed the most unforgivable crime of all time. I prayed I would not be called upon to make any such desperate decision. To prepare for eventualities I decided to change into uniform, so rang for my steward.

'Are we nearly in, sire?' Squires enquired hopefully. He loathed the sea and, as he seldom went on deck, he never had any idea where we were.

'Very nearly indeed, I should say,' I replied.

'What a quick trip, sire!'

'It might be the quickest ever...in fact any minute now,' I added rather sinisterly. 'The question is where are we bound for? I can't see you with a harp and a halo.'

'I wish you wouldn't say things like that, sire,' Squires said petulantly. 'It upsets me.'

'Upset could be right,' I told him.

Squires looked surreptitiously at the bottle rack, but, as we were at sea, it was empty, so he concentrated his energies on brushing my uniform.

The next day we picked up a signal *en clair* to say that H.M.S. *Hood* had been sunk—but no position was given.

I sent for Haliday and we went over his latest intelligence. I felt worried about the battle which must be going on to the west of us. Haliday told me that from the frenzied wireless activity on the air he calculated that a German battle squadron was at large and engaging heavy British ships. Now the news of the loss of H.M.S. *Hood* was official. I had a conference with my officers and explained the difficulty of our own position. We decided not to have any regular watches, but to camp out on the bridge. The next three days were our own private nightmare; the fog became worse and our best chance of detecting heavy ships in our vicinity lay in listening in on our hydrophones and keeping our eyes skinned.

I didn't say anything to the other escorts or the Commodore, for I felt that if I suggested we were in danger I might get a false sighting report from them, which would only confuse matters.

When we were within a hundred miles of Iceland, on 27th May, we received the following signal:

FROM C.-IN-C. HOME FLEET

BISMARCK SUNK

T.O.O. 1040/17/5

Distribution—All ships and submarines at sea.

After a terrific fight this gallant ship had met her death some thousand miles away from us, in about 48°10′N and 16°10′W.

I am not sure who was the more relieved, Squires or myself. I know I gave the order to 'splice the mainbrace', which included having a private Scotch with Squires, who was above drinking naval rum. I won a slight personal victory over Squires on this occasion, as, instead of saying 'God Bless' as we raised our glasses to drink, I said, *'Non nobis solum.'*

Squires replied, 'I've never visited that place, sire.'

On arrival in Iceland, having said farewell to the Commodore and made the necessary signals, I decided to anchor in the roads for two reasons. Firstly, I wanted to do captain's rounds, and secondly to censor the ship's mail before it went ashore. We had arrived on a Saturday and I informed Turner I would inspect the ship on Sunday, after church service at 1100. Divine service at sea was, to me, always an emotional and uplifting experience. As C.O., I took the service and chose the prayers. Aided by the ship's band, we sang those beautiful and stirring hymns, 'Eternal Farther, strong to save' and 'Abide with me'.

When inspecting one's ship, one knows from experience as a junior officer that it is a friendly contest which might well be called

'The C.O. *v.* The Rest.' In my case, the opposing centre-forward was Turner, ably backed up by Sloane, the leading seaman, Donald, Blundell, Gaunt, Glue, the chief and the second engineer. Captain's rounds with No.1 in attendance consisted of a conducted tour though the ship. In the seamen's mess everything is for once in a while the acme of tidiness. Kit and ditty-boxes laid out, hammocks furled, oilskins and sea-boots in their lockers and the men themselves clean and immaculately dressed. I didn't really pay much attention to these things, it was the human side of the crew's lives which interested me—the photographs of their sweethearts, wives and children, and the crude and often pathetic keepsakes, which meant so much to them. The stokers' mess in any ship is always the cleanest, which is very understandable, but it also almost always contains a definite type of pin-up girls pasted on to the bulkheads. These females resembled scantily clad 'can-can' girls, they were arrayed in tight, black-lace underwear and had 'protruding upperworks' and 'bulging sterns'. It was Rochefoucald, I think, who said: *'Le travail du corps délivre des peines de l'esprit et c'est ce que rend les pauvres heureux.'*

However, on captain's rounds, a C.O.'s job is to look under the carpet. Therefore I inspected the seamen's 'heads', scrutinized the pots and pans in the galley and invaded the bosun's store. I enjoyed most the visit to the engine-room. I was fascinated by this world, where steam faintly hissed and the stationary machinery shone like an exhibition model. The gauges, the polished wheels, the steel gratings and the smell of oil intrigued me. The boilers and the stoke hole I can only describe as a large edition of a railway locomotive. The stoking is the same, but when the ship is rolling 40 degrees or pitching violently in heavy seas it becomes an art. To make sure of this, I had tried it myself.

When on this particular Sunday captain's rounds were duly completed, Turner invited me to the C.P.O's mess—as is traditional. The amusing part of this act is that one is offered the ship's rum and various other drinks, in spite of the fact that the K.R. and

MY SEA LADY

A.I. lay down that no alcoholic drinks are ever to be available to the crew other than the daily 'up spirits' rum ration, which must be consumed on the spot in the presence of an officer. P.O.s drink in their own mess but are not supposed to bottle their rum ration.

Our homeward trip was an astonishing one, as for some strange reason we were routed inside the Vestmanaeyja. We were due to sail at noon, but, as there was a dense fog at sea, I suggested we delayed sailing, but N.S.C.O. thought otherwise, so off we went into the murk and promptly lost touch with the convoy and the other escorts. Getting through the 'hole in the wall' at Reykjanes is bad enough at any time, but in a fog it is asking for trouble. A day later, visibility was about half a mile. The first thing we saw was one of the Vestmanaeyja, which are really huge volcanic rocks rising sheer out of the water to a height of about 1,000 ft. This string of 'islands' stretches to seaward and there is only one navigable channel, which is between the beach and the first rock. I had no idea which of the rocks we had sighted, so decided to sail towards the short and risk running aground. It was getting daylight, and through the fog we say the breakers in time, but I wouldn't care to try to do it at night.

At the time I kept wondering how the other ships had fared, and was glad next day we came up with one of the merchant ships which we were supposed to be escorting! The captain told me he had gone straight out to sea from Recky and not taken any notice of the steeplechase course laid down by N.S.C.O. We sailed in company with him, and did not see the rest of our party until a week later, when we all collected in the Minches. I felt rather upset about this convoy (I was S.O.), but lost no time in making a signal to C.-in-C. W.A. to say the convoy had 'arrived safely'. I would have liked to have said 'the convoy got through', but in this case our only enemy had been N.S.C.O.'s crazy routing and his instructions to sail in a thick fog.

On reaching the Clyde, we were ordered by the Gourock signal station to go alongside a Polish destroyer named *Burza*. When we were tied up her captain asked me aboard (it was about 0930) and enquired if I knew C.-in-C. W.A. was inspecting both our ships at about noon that very day.

The C.O. of the *Burza* showed me a lot of orders from the base, stating what we were expected to do, and it was quite clear to me that he had less idea than I had as to what we were in for. I dashed back to *Lady M* and broke the news to No.1 and prayed that the ship could be scrubbed out in time. To tie up at 0900 after an ocean passage, and be inspected by your C.-in-C. at noon, does not leave much time for cleaning ship and putting on the spit and polish. However, I did not then appreciate that I had the joker up my sleeve in the form of Turner.

At about 1000 'Guns' came down from Greenock to tell us how to receive an admiral, and also to coach the Poles. 'Guns' explained that D was sorry to put us into such a spot, but that C.-in-C. W.A. had insisted on inspecting a trawler and we were the only one in the port. (The story of our encounter with the U-boat was also in circulation.) I cleared the lower deck and told the hands that Commander-in-Chief Western Approaches had expressed a special wish to inspect our ship, and this was about the greatest honour that could be bestowed upon *Lady Madeleine*, so we must work for the next two hours as we had never worked before. We did. I took off my jacket, rolled up my sleeves and turned to. The crew were enthusiastic and by 1130, when it was time to get into our No. 1s, as Turner said, '*Lady M* looks a fair treat.' Sir Percy Noble first boarded the Polish ship, and I understand that the routine in the Polish Navy is that the inspecting admiral goes aboard and then says, 'Bless you, my children,' whereupon the ship's company yell back a battle-cry. Anyhow, whatever C.-in-C. W.A. said, the Poles let go a war-whoop and then permitted him to inspect their ship. I stood shivering at my gangway, supported by Geoff and the coxswain. Half an hour later Sir Percy was piped aboard *Lady M*, followed by Admiral Watson (F.O.I.C. Greenock) and our Captain D. He inspected the ship—the coxswain much in evidence, skilfully leading the way—and finally made a speech to the ship's company, which made us all feel like heroes. I know when I called for three cheers for our C.-in-C. (not to be outdone by the Poles) the noise must have been heard in Glasgow.

After the inspection I lunched with the Poles, and if you have not had this delightful experience I may as well tell you that you come to some time the next day.

O ur next convoy took us out west again, but this time we had a stranger as Senior Officer, who was not part of the Clyde A/S Escort Force, so when we went off to hunt suspicious 'contacts' he could not understand it at all. One evening we got a very strong contact between our ship and the convoy. I turned the ship to attack and had to steam down the side of the port column of ships. I do not know if we were on to a U-boat or not, but there was every indication of it, so we let go with our depth-charges at the appropriate moment. I was so interested in making an accurate attack that I got too close to the convoy, with the result that the port thrower sent a depth-charge almost alongside one of the merchant ships. Thank God the charge did not explode! Fortunately for me, the S.O. did not notice my over-enthusiasm, but it taught me a lesson.

The rest of this trip was uneventful. I always mistrust the word 'uneventful'. It's like 'laconic' and 'mopping up', which usually spell disaster. During this we spent most of the time trying to read the S.O.'s flag-hoists and got sick to death of him. When the time came to leave this convoy and return to our base I was anxious to make a suitable parting signal to him. Somebody hastily produced some seaman's underwear and so I told the signalman to bend these on to the signal halyard and hoist them. I then steamed up to our friend to be sure he saw our signal.

We were not very far from base at the time and got back to Greenock the same day during daylight, cutting the corner at

Pladda light and 'shaking hands with the lighthouse keeper's daughter'.

As we were going alongside, my signalman enquired if he should fly the knickers 'close up' or 'at the dip'. That started the myth about 'Lady M's knickers', which led to a lot of fun. The joke went the rounds of the base and several very charming young ladies, misinterpreting the situation, gave us some 'spare pennants'. Lady M got quite dressy. There are a number of flags which are not listed in the naval signal books. A purple flag with yellow spots on it means 'take no notice of my actions, I'm tight', or a pink flag with a hole in it means 'will swop a case of gin for a blonde'.

In September there was a general reorganization of the Clyde Escort Force. It was decided to form special trawler groups, which would escort the smaller and slower merchant ships on Atlantic and Icelandic convoys. *Lady M, Arab, Ayrshire, Notts County, Norwich City*, and later *St. Loman*, were formed into the 49th Group. There was Leo Gradwell, Clem Shillan, Hampden, Uncle Stammers and myself.

We met in my cabin in *Lady M* to discuss the situation, and christened ourselves 'The Fighting 49th'. I said to Leo that 'The Fighting 49th' sounded to me more like a cavalry regiment on the North-West Frontier than a trawler group. He agreed, and asked, 'Was it Poonah or Delhi when we won the polo cup?' From that moment the '49th' became very horsy. I was the colonel, as this appeared to be the only way to get promotion in the sea-going end of the R.N.V.R. I promoted the others, as I thought it was about time we ceased to be lieutenants. Captain D gave a cocktail party to celebrate these new arrangements, and so I told 'the regiment' we would attend in mess dress.

As everybody knows, all cavalry officers sport the most fierce moustaches, and when we put in an appearance at D's party the officers of 'The Fighting 49th' would have scared the daylight out of any tribesman. Leo had an immense square affair, and as the colonel I wore a grey 'drooper'. When we first appeared there was an ominous silence, so I informed D that as the '49th' was a cavalry regiment we had come to draw our horses. Much gin and laughter followed. Better still, we were given leave.

Unexpected leave always throws any ship's company into a high state of confusion. Out of three watches, two are normally due for leave, but quite naturally in a case like this everybody considers it is his turn and request-men seem to be everywhere. Geoff and I tried to sort out the situation, while Bill wrote out the railway warrants and Mac tried to keep track of what we were doing, as he, poor fellow, had drawn the folded paper out of the hat which had 'Duty Officer' written on it. He and one duty watch would have to stay in the ship.

For once I had managed to get myself a sleeper on the night train to London, and as I lay down in the dark listening to the coach wheels go 'clickety-click, chugity-chug', I prayed that my telegram had reached Sally's flat in time to warn her of my intended arrival—that was if she was in London at all. It was now the end of the summer of 1941. I had been away at sea and not been south since early in 1940.

I wondered what London would be like after the blitz and the great fire of 10th May, when I had read the city had burned more fiercely than it had done 275 years earlier. London, I imagined, must be a city in a state of siege, its inhabitants stunned and its very life in the balance.

As the train stopped at Carlisle in the small hours of the morning, I heard the clank of the milk-churns and sleepy voices drifting down the corridor. In a dreamy way thoughts about my time at sea drifted through my mind. Not the remorseless battle of the Atlantic, but the moments of beauty which had also been part of my life. 'Call me at first light,' I had said so often to the officer of the watch and, coming on to the bridge, I had seen the fading stars and the brightening dawn. In calm weather it was the utter silence of the new day which was so enthralling; the sea would be like milk beneath a lightening sky, then, when the sun began to creep over the horizon, the whole atmosphere became charged with luminous gold. If we were near the ice edge its pastel-blue peaks were tinted rose colour by the rising sun. At night the northern lights illuminated the seascape with a weird, flickering brilliance. With such thoughts in my head I drifted off to sleep— when I awoke it was broad daylight and the train was at Euston. The station clock had stopped, but my wrist watch told me it was 0600. In the pale morning sunlight the whole scene was hushed and deserted. The platforms were piled high with mail-sacks, wooden boxes, crates of vegetables and milk-cans. I found some hot water in the station washrooms, shaved and tried to smarten myself up before searching for a taxi. In the end I had to walk to Mill Street, arriving there about 0730. Sally had a flat on the third floor, and without thinking I climbed the stairs to her door. There on the mat lay a telegram. I was sure it was my telegram, but didn't open it. I left the orange envelope where it was and went back down the creaking stairs to the street. Outside it was warm and sunny, but now I felt deflated and miserable. For all I knew Sally might be a hundred miles away, but the windows of her flat were open, so I sat down on the pavement to wait. After the train journey and the walk, having had nothing to eat or drink for twelve hours, I was tired and so dropped off to sleep. The next thing I knew was that I was the centre of attention for a small group of bystanders. I heard a milkman say, 'You'd better hurry up, guv'nor, or you'll be late.' I got to my feet rather stiffly, and then saw the joke. While I had slumbered, Sally had seen me from across the road and come down to 'make an inspection'. She had decided not to wake me and had written in bright-red lipstick on the pavement beside me: 'Breakfast served 8.45 sharp—Sally.' Somewhere a clock struck nine.

While Sally had her hair done, I walked to the National Provincial Bank in Trafalgar Square to get some money and see my long-suffering friend Mr. Brunton, the manager. The London I saw was very different from the London I had known. The first shock was the posters which read: 'Careless Talk costs lives', 'Is your journey really necessary?', 'Don't be a food hog', 'Give a woman your place in the shelter' and 'Britain can take it'. 'Take what?' I thought to myself. This was a fine sort of story.

London's leafy squares now had strange elongated trees stretching into the sky, known as the balloon barrage. At Marble Arch, Hyde Park Corner and in Green Park I saw the A.A. gun-sites and their tired tin-hatted crews. The streets were curiously empty and when the sirens wailed their warning note they seemed to die altogether. I walked on, steering a south-westerly course, but was accosted by an A.A. warden who informed me I should be wearing a tin hat and that the nearest shelter was the Green Park Tube station. I went into the nearest public house. I hadn't got a tin hat or a gasmask. After the 'all clear' I found Mr. Brunton and thanked him for cashing cheques from here, there and everywhere. I could never have survived without the 'N.P.' and Mr. Brunton. He was desperately interested in the war and had a large map on his office wall. This showed the extent of the German advance into Russia and their conquest of Europe. It presented a sinister and frightening picture. Our little island seemed terribly alone, but Mr. Brunton, who had fought in the Kaiser's War, was not down-hearted. He collected empty shell cases and I promised to provide him with some from the *Lady M*'s guns. Later on the staff of this most excellent bank adopted *Lady M* as their warship, and provided myself and the crew with all sorts of ship's comforts, ranging from clothing to books, magazines and gramophone records.

After leaving Brunton I crossed the road and dived into the secret depths of the Admiralty. It is hard to believe, but they had an excellent bar down there, where one might meet people like Admiral Clayton, Humphrey Sandwith, Barrow Green, Ian Fleming, Guy Hughes, Roger Winn, Malcolm Saunders, Walter Westhead, Peter Kemp and even D.N.I. (Admiral Godfrey) himself. I gathered that, although the gin was holding out, our position at sea was a pretty desperate one.

If you take off time for travelling, my leave amounted to only forty-eight hours, so time slipped away all too quickly. Sally was playing at the Duke of Devonshire Theatre and I spent quite a lot of time there. The show was packed in spite of the bombs, air-raid warnings and raids. 'The show must go on', and go on it did.

We had supper and danced at Hatchett's. The restaurant being below street level, the sound of gun-fire and exploding bombs failed to drown the orchestra—it would take more than that to keep Chappie D'Amato's band quiet.

I had grown accustomed to the darkness of the sea, but the London blackout distressed me. It was like being confined inside a vast black box with a few pin-pricks for light. After the wideness of the sea it gave me a feeling of claustrophobia. Next day I inspected the damage done by the German bombs. St. Pancras 'wasn't there', Victoria Station was a shambles. The Café de Paris had had it, so had the Carlton Hotel; the Alexandra Hotel in Knightsbridge was a wreck and so were many other buildings, including my club. I even saw the skeleton of some prehistoric monster hanging out of a window of the Kensington Natural History Museum.

I said farewell to Sally, and once again heard the milk-churns rattle at Carlisle as the train sped northwards.

But all through the night I was restless and unable to sleep. I finished the contents of my small flask, hoping the wartime whisky would help, but drinking it only served to remind me of a line from Swinburne...'for dead men deadly wine'. That started me thinking about the old superstition that a sailor drowns if a wine glass is allowed to ring. Then for hours the whole train seemed to ring like a gigantic glass and yet I was powerless to stop it. I also had the uncomfortable feeling I wasn't alone in my sleeper and that I could easily guess my companion's identity. When the train arrived in daylight at Glasgow, feeling bolder I bade my unseen visitor goodbye—but I didn't expect it would be for long as in those days death was seldom far away from me.

L ife for the '49th' turned out to be a very grim affair, since winter in the North Atlantic is a battle against the elements. Now we had the task of being responsible for the safety of many millions of pounds' worth of merchant shipping. If anything went wrong the blame would fall on me.

Lady M spent the next three months thrashing about the northern Atlantic, tormented by cruel seas and howling gales. The weather was so fierce that we often had to lie to for days, and celestial navigation was impossible—even Hampden, who was a professional navigator, used to get lost.

Celestial navigation is all very well, but if you do not see either the sun, moon or stars for days on end it is not of much help.

On one trip we made the Commodore's ship was a 7,000-tonner called *P.L.M.II*. We had such a foul passage to Iceland that we had to lie to for days, got separated from one another and I am sorry to say two small merchant ships never arrived at all. Leo fetched up miles up the coast north of Akranes; I staggered to Recky with the Commodore, and little by little the other escorts and merchant ships arrived, all having sustained severe damage from the weather. When I saw the Commodore ashore I said to him: 'What a lousy trip. Were you all right?'

'Well, all my lights went out,' he said, 'and I had to navigate and steer by a candle, as the lamp oil gave out too. I didn't mind that so much, the thing that worried me was whether you in your cockleshell would ever live in such a sea. I never thought you would make it.' What a man! We were supposed to be protecting him. Captain Smith came aboard *Lady M* and we celebrated the convoy's arrival by sharing a bottle of whisky.

While the snow was flopping steadily on to *Lady M*'s deck, the Commodore and I sat in the warmth of my cabin drinking and yarning. After some while, he pulled a battered newspaper from his pocket and shoved it at me. 'Read that,' he grunted. 'It fairly well makes me sick.' The paper was dated 30th September 1938. I read the passage he had marked in the leading article:

> People of Britain, your children are safe. You husbands and your sons will not march to battle. A war which would have been the most criminal, the most futile, the most destructive that ever insulted the purposes of the Almighty and the intelligence of men has been averted.
>
> It was the war that nobody wanted. Nobody in Germany. Nobody in France. Nobody, above all, in Britain, which had no concern whatever with the issues at stake.

I put the paper down in disgust. 'Death in a top-hat,' I suggested.

'Say what you like,' said Smith, 'but it won't alter the fact that here we are fighting tooth and nail for our very existence, while the Germans have conquered Europe.'

'Well, the only chance of mental survival is to forget about it,' I said. 'Let's have another nip and read the sporting news on the 30th September 1938. Here, give me the paper.

This is what I discovered. Michoumy was a 9-1 favourite for

the Cambridgeshire and it was 100-8 against Black Spec for the Cesarewitch. Chelsea were playing Stoke City and the Arsenal were up against Sutherland. Tyrone Power and Alice Faye had just completed a film called *Alexander's Ragtime Band*. A glance at the City page told me that the Stock Exchange had leaped ahead and I noticed that British American Tobacco shares were nearly a pound up at 100*s*. and Imperial Tobacco were ten bob better at around 140*s*. This made me think of that old parody:

> "Twas on a springtime afternoon,
> Old Gasper's work was done,
> And W.D. and H.O. Wills
> Were sitting in the sun.'

Well, Lieutenant W.G. Ogden, R.N.V.R., was freezing to death in the Icelandic gloom. We came to the conclusion it would be all the same in a hundred years' time, so retired to a drunken slumber.

The homeward trip was just about as bad. We took some ships from Recky, and the idea was to join up with an east-bound convoy from Halifax.

The weather was so filthy that we never all got together until we were nearly home. The whole escort and convoy were strung out over the ocean. *Lady M* would spend one night with a batch of ships and then go and find some more bedfellows. We did this for 700 miles. The weather was appalling. Great angry seas hissed past us, piling up into murderous waves. *Lady M* would slide down their huge rollers, as if she was intent on plunging to the bottom of the sea, but at the last minute her flared bows would lift her and she would start to climb the next green watery hill. The demented shriek of the wind and the ever-threatening sky haunted us. We were driving ourselves and our ship to a point of exhaustion.

In small ships rough weather puts a terrific strain on everybody and everything. It is almost impossible to stand up without hanging on to something the whole time. Feeding is an effort and necessitates judging the roll or pitch of the ship and holding on to whatever is nearest with one hand and trying to eat with the other. Hot food is out of the question. We lived on bully-beef and biscuits.

Most trawler wardrooms get waterlogged in heavy weather, as water comes hurtling down the bogey stove pipe and out goes the fire in a cloud of steam. The deck-head invariably leaks because the trawler 'fish-hold' was never intended to house humans and the ventilators, besides providing air, provide a stream of salt-water. I hear somebody say, 'Well, turn them to the lee side, and put canvas over them,' but my answer is that when you were 'green seas over' it didn't make much difference, the water came in just the same. In rough weather I had to wedge myself into my bunk. This is such a complicated manœuvre that I can't really explain it. The pieces of the puzzle were the mattress, two inflated Mae Wests, two cushions, a pillow, the ship's cat and yours truly.

On one of the few nights when I was sound asleep in my bunk I had to tear up to the bridge in my pyjamas, as we had run into another convoy. Bleary-eyed, I ordered the quartermaster to put the helm hard over. We then indulged in a series of violent swerves. Young Blundell was on the wheel with Donald in attendance, so I was able to stand outside on the lower bridge and give the helm orders from there until we were out of our troubles. That's what you get for turning in at sea and undressing.

Looking at *Lady M*'s logbook, I see that it was on this convoy that at 2200 on 7th December 1941 we picked up the following signal from Their Lordships addressed to:

C.-IN-C. AMERICA AND WEST INDIES
COMMENCE HOSTILITIES AGAINST JAPAN
REPEAT JAPAN AT ONCE
2143A/7

I liked the 'at once' part of the signal. What were we supposed to do? Geoff was bubbling over with joy.

'That means the Yanks are in the war,' he said.

'I don't see why,' I said.

'It couldn't mean anything else. The Japs must have attacked them, otherwise what's it all about?'

How right he was. Pearl Harbour, the Jap carriers, suicide Kamikaze dive-bombers, the devastation of the U.S. Pacific fleet at anchor and the ghastly realization by the people of the U.S.A. of this treacherous act.

'You think we're all right now?' I asked him.

'We are bound to win now,' Geoff laughed. 'We can't go wrong.'

However, the next signals I saw were not so comforting. They were from the U-boat Intelligence Section at the Admiralty, presided over by my old friend Roger Winn. They gave us his estimated positions of the U-boats at sea, and on this occasion some pretty near our route.

I reproduce here a typical example of one of these intelligence reports:

SECRET   NAVAL MESSAGE   IMMEDIATE

U-boat situation Report N.E. Atlantic

C.-in-C. U.S. Fleet   V Admty

Aircraft sighting at 1422-27th August indicates 1 U-boat patrolling in North Minches.

Similar operations in other inshore areas such as North Channel are accordingly considered probable. Several U-boats are estimated outward bound North of British Isles, probably scattered between South-West Iceland and North-West Ireland and Norwegian Coast.

No fresh information since D/F 03072 26th August or 3 or 4 probably now Northbound between MM 30 and CV 30 and MS and TY (47°30′N and 52°30′N and 16°W and 21°W).

Part 2. final About 15 outward bound between SV (12°W) and Bay of Biscay ports.

2 or 3 on passage within 120 miles.

When we were next in port Clem Shillan, the C.O. of *Arab* and I decided to go to Glasgow to see a theatre.

We dined early at Rogano's, and tried to get seats for Ivor Novello's show, *The Dancing Years*. There wasn't a seat to be had. I knew Novello, so we went backstage to see if anything could be arranged. Ivor was, as usual, his charming self and suggested the only thing to do was to see the show from the wings.

'Nothing better,' we said, 'thanks very much.'

In the next hour we took a lot of unexpected exercise. Every time we sat down scene-shifters would whisk away whatever we were sitting on, which, to our surprise, turned out to be anything from the moon to a castle turret. There was one big scene of Austrian peasants and army officers, so we joined the back row of the chorus. Clem's voice is good on the bridge, but I didn't care for it so much 'on the boards'.

Later, when the curtain was rung down, the cast went off to their dressing-rooms, so I said to Clem I thought it was probably half-time. He suggested we should soothe our nerves by going to the bar, to prepare us for greater activities in the second act. In order to do this we had to cross the stage. Well, it had to happen. While in mid-stage we suddenly saw the footlights go on. I was so surprised, all I noticed was that they were reds, whites and blues. I also saw the curtain slowly rising. We ran for it, but the audience saw the lower halves of two naval officers travelling at speed across the stage and applauded loudly. We apologized to Ivor, and spent the rest of the performance in the bar discussing our theatrical career.

F rom the following reports of proceedings on convoy U.R.2 it will be seen that we arrived at Reykjavik on Christmas Day 1941.

To: THE CAPTAIN (D) GREENOCK
From: THE COMMANDING OFFICER, H.M.T. *Lady Madeleine*
Date: 4th January 1942

REPORT OF PROCEEDINGS ON U.R.2 AND R.U.2.

1.   After leaving Loch Ewe on 2100 on December 19th, with ten motor vessels, *Notts County* and *Coventry City*, we ran into a heavy westerly gale, and *Lady Madeleine* was obliged to heave to for about twelve hours, some fifty miles north west of the Butt. The convoy was joined next day and proceeded in bad weather.

2.   However, on the 23rd *Notts County* and *Norwich City* lost the convoy in heavy weather and poor visibility, and were not able to rejoin before Reykjanes. The convoy arrived safely A.M. on 25th December.

The points of interest of this trip are:

(1)   that the weather and visibility are at times so bad that it would be of the greatest value to the escorts if they were fitted with R.D.F.,

(2)   M/F D/F would be an advantage for navigational purposes (apart from getting bearings from U-boats on 384 kc/s).

(3)   In order to make a safe landfall approaching Iceland an Echo Sounder is essential, as the chance of getting a position from the sun, moon or stars may not occur for days on end. Similarly, the local magnetic disturbances definitely affect the ship's compasses.

> (Signed) GRAEME OGDEN
> Lieutenant R.N.V.R.

REPORT OF PROCEEDINGS ON U.R.2 AND R.U.2

(The Commanding Officer, H.M.T. *Lady Madeleine*'s report dated 4th January 1942)

II

No. 8032/191

THE COMMANDER-IN-CHIEF, WESTERN APPROACHES

Copy to:

> *The Commanding Officer, H.M.T. Lady Madeleine*
> Forwarded.

1.   Points of interest (1) and (2) are concurred in, and it is suggested that Type 271 R.D.F. or a kindred set should be fitted in trawlers of the Ocean Escort Forces.

2.   The priority of all trawlers being fitted with M/F D/F must of necessity be low, but it is considered desirable to fit the ships of Senior Officers of Trawler Groups with M/F D/F as soon as sets are available.

3.   It is also considered desirable that certain trawlers should be ear-marked for Senior Officer's duties in these Groups, since it may well be desirable to give them priority in various forms of equipment. It is undesirable that, as a result of a Commanding Officer being relieved, that particular trawler should become a comparatively junior member of her group.

4.   With reference to Point of Interest (3), the question of echo sounding machines in trawlers is being investigated.

(Signed) S.V. JEPHSON
CAPTAIN (D) GREENOCK

Naval Offices,
Albert Harbour
Greenock, 13th January 1942

But just how we got there is a different story. As you can well imagine, both merchantmen and escorts were anxious to make the passage on or before the 25th, so that Christmas Day could be spent in comfort in harbour and not thrashing about in the icy seas outside. Steering a north-westerly course, we urged our ships forward like jockeys with the whip out entering the finishing straight. We encountered snow-squalls and the temperature fell to below freezing point.

Our difficulty lay, as always, in trying to make a landfall. We were without modern navigational instruments, and had to rely on our eyesight to pick up the Icelandic coast. The best chance was to try and sight the top of the Myrdals Glacier, which is nearly 4,000 ft. high, but naturally you can see this only in daylight. Otherwise, one has to go by soundings and trust to luck. In this case, we sighted the cape at Vik in what passed for daylight, and crept along the coast to Selfois and round the corner to the light at Skagaflös and on to Recky. By good luck, the convoy arrived in Recky Roads about noon on Christmas Day. Having informed the base of our presence, I made a signal for the convoy and escorts 'to disperse'— in other words it was every man for himself to get alongside if he could.

Recky is just north of latitude 64 and up there in wintertime there are only a few hours of sickly daylight, resembling a pink chalk smudge on a blackboard sky. I took *Lady M* straight into the inner harbour without saying 'anything to anyone', for if I had requested a berth I knew I would have been told to anchor in the roads. It was now snowing heavily and there was a stiff off-shore wind and as there was no empty berth in sight when I entered the harbour I stopped *Lady M*'s engines and left the rest to her. She chose to fetch up alongside an American freighter called *Wichita Falls*. I could always trust *Lady M* to do the right thing and on this occasion she excelled herself for her Christmas choice, since her bedfellow turned out to be loaded with canned beer for the U.S.A. forces now arriving in Iceland.

I found the American skipper of *Wichita Falls* a most delightful fellow, and it was not long before our crews had joined up together for their Christmas dinner of American canned turkey.

Next day, feeling more relaxed and in a better temper, I had to admit to myself that Recky, with its snow-covered buildings and twinkling lights, was not so bad after all. The cold, however, was so intense that ice began to form on the steel bulkheads of my cabin in spite of two electric heaters.

On visiting A.C.I.C. (Admiral Commanding Icelandic Command), I learned we were to sail home with convoy R.U.6 on Friday, 16th January 1942. However, a lot was to happen before we sailed, as I will tell you, and can also be seen from my report to Captain D. Greenock. In the forenoon of 15th January the wind freshened. We were now in the Roads and had shortened to about six shackles of anchor cable, in readiness for sailing, and everything appeared to be under control. However, the wind continued to rise and the glass fell alarmingly. At noon it was blowing a full gale from the north-east. I said to Geoff I didn't like the spite in the wind, and thought the best thing we could do was to get up the hook and go out to sea. The holding ground in Recky Roads is chancy. Some people say the bottom's made of volcanic stone, others say it's highly polished marble. I am inclined to the marble theory, for, as I was discussing the situation with Geoff, *Lady M* gave a lurch, dragged her anchor and went careering off downwind towards Engg Island. We were not on a lee shore, otherwise we shouldn't have had a chance. The gust which started *Lady M* off caused a corvette to crash into a trawler and, narrowly missing us, they both waltzed off downwind together. The roads were full of shipping, and it looked as if we were bound to crash into something in our headlong dash seawards. I had to go full ahead to keep steerage way on *Lady M*, and remembering we still had six shackles of anchor cable streaming behind us. We got some of it in, but our hectic dash was halted when we wrapped our hook firmly round a Dutchman's anchor cable.

Lady M proceeded to go stern to wind, as a trawler will do if out of control in a high wind. The wind had now reached hurricane force, and by going full astern I could just keep *Lady M* clear. The problem was to keep her astern of the Dutchman without hitting him. We remained where we were for about an hour, and I prayed that the wind would go away or veer a little and let me slide down his port side. The glass, however, continued to fall and the harbour was a sheet of flying spray. The wind was now so strong that it cut the tops off the waves and the outer harbour became a whirlpool of foam. The sky was dark purple and the sea a deep brownish colour. I decided that we were not simply foul of the Dutchman, but that our hook must have got round something else—possibly an old cable on the bottom—and in addition the bight of our anchor cable was round his. Trawlers carry twelve shackles of anchor cable, that is to say 180 fathoms, so we calculated that if we let go another five shackles we might bring up astern of the Dutchman or else drag our anchor. I didn't think that was likely, though, because it appeared to be pretty firmly home into something or other. The difficulty was that once we slackened the dog on the winch the cable would then take charge and either snap or run out altogether. We decided to use the engines to take the strain, and to take advantage of the least slackening of the wind slowly to ease away the cable. It wasn't as easy as it sounds, for by now the wind had reached a speed of about ninety miles an hour. The fo'c'sle party could not stand up, owing to the force of the wind, and were hardly visible to me through the flying spray; even signs were difficult to see. Our giant leading seaman, Paddy Sloan, who was lying on the foredeck, eased away the cable, and eventually we found ourselves head to wind astern of the Dutchman. To stay in this position, of course, we had to steam ahead, and at times full ahead. I think the hurricane reached its height at about 1800 when its official speed ashore was given as 120 miles per hour. I spent my time crawling down from the bridge to my cabin to look at my barometer. About that time it showed 26·4. This was the lowest I have ever seen it. Water was now driving past the bridge (which is 27 ft. above sea-level) in a solid sheet. I couldn't see the sky, and I couldn't see the surface of the sea. *Lady M* veered about on her cable like a frightened animal, and I expected her to break loose at any minute. God knows what would have happened if she had, because a mass of shipping was piling up between us and the open sea.

The effect of the hurricane, when it was at its height, was like being in a tunnel. It was impossible to stand up, and the only way one could see anything at all was by putting one's face into the large end of the hand megaphone and quickly squinting through it.

According to the log, my barometer started to rise about 2200 and the wind began to go away. We spent a most uncomfortable night, with *Lady M* still yawing about like a mad thing, but in the morning we were still astern of the Dutchman, and there was only a fresh breeze blowing. When daylight came, about 1100 in the morning, the outer harbour and roads presented a most peculiar sight.

The roads were dotted with groups of shipping of all varieties, which had got foul of one another during the night—cargo ships, tankers, escorts, were all tangled up together. More amazing still, there were twenty ships ashore. Wherever you looked you saw ships apparently rising out of fields. I had never seen anything like it before, and hope I never shall again, because that hurricane did more damage to our shipping than any amount of U-boats. The last time I was in Recky in 1943 some of those ships were still ashore.

Our problem, like everyone else's, was to 'undo the knitting'— that is to say, clear our anchor and cable. This proved easier than I had thought, and we must have been lucky, because in a few hours we were clear and had tied up alongside the Dutchman. I went aboard and apologized for having crashed his moorings, but the Dutch captain wouldn't listen. He said he had been worried to death about us and had had to steam full ahead on his anchors all the previous day and night. He filled me up with Bols, and suggested we stay alongside him that night. We were only too pleased, and accepted. We slept all next day, having first ascertained that our own storm damage was very slight—we had, in fact, only knocked off our Asdic dome. We had this repaired and sailed home with R.U.6.

One of the best stories of the Big Blow was that an air-force officer rang up the naval base and reported 'one Nissen hut just airborne, flying in your direction' and then rang off. Strange as it seems now, Nissen huts were actually flying about that night.

When on 19th January R.U.7 did sail we soon ran into bad weather. A westerly gale developed and, as our course was approximately south-east, this put the wind on our quarter (which is always a good place to have it, for although it will drive one to the south, this can be allowed for). I said to Geoff that if the wind held we should make a fast passage. We were both keen to get back to base, as *Lady M* was at last to refit. This meant a good spell of leave, and also getting a lot of alterations and improvements done to the ship.

The wind held for the next two days, but there was a big sea running. The Commodore's ship, *Lysaker*, developed some engine-room defect and was forced to slow down to 6 knots, so we were ordered to stay behind with her while the others cracked on homewards. That night it blew harder still, and when daylight came there was no sign of the Commodore. The sun came out and we got a sight and checked our position, which agreed with our D.R., and I reckoned we were about 200 miles west of Tory Island. About noon we altered course to due east, which put the sea dead astern of us.

It was now blowing a full gale and the seas were towering behind us. With a following sea, if you regulate your ship's speed to that of the sea you don't notice the size of the waves so much, but from crest to trough I calculated these waves were about 30 ft. high.

REPORT OF PROCEEDINGS

U.R.6 and R.U.7.
6th Jan. 1942 to 26th

To: CAPTAIN (D) GREENOCK
From: COMMANDING OFFICER, *Lady Madeleine*

1. I sailed from Greenock at 0700/6 and arrived off Aultbea Pier at 0900/7. In spite of continual efforts I was unable to get a boat off we did *not* attend N.C.S.O.'s Conference—I eventually got ashore afterwards and extracted my sailing orders.

2. The convoy consisted of 5 M/V's and the escort of *Ayrshire, Norwich City* and *Lady Madeleine*.

3. The weather was bad going North and some 40 miles South-East of Iceland, the Commodore in P.L.M.14 decided to heave to. I stood by him that night but the convoy became scattered. Next morning I informed Admiral Commanding Iceland (C).

4. The next morning, Sunday January 11th, we all attempted to make Reykjavik via Reykjanes. The weather worsened and later it blew a hurricane (80 knots). The result was that *Coventry City* arrived with 2 ships on the 12th, we arrived at 1600 on the 12th having nearly gone ashore at Akranes earlier in the day. The Commodore limped in p.m. on the 13th and *Ayrshire* on the 14th. 2 M/V's also arrived but 1 M/V, the *Reias*, is thought to have been lost.

5. R.U.6 was due to sail a.m. Friday 16th, but during Thursday night it blew very hard while we were all at anchor and in the morning it blew a hurricane at over 100 knots from the South East.

THE NARRATIVE 75

6.   Almost every ship dragged her anchors. We fouled an M/V and our cable carried away our dome. The wind eased at 2045 but the next day, 16th January, there were 10 ships ashore at Reykjavik and 6 at Hvalfiord.

7.   R.U.6 sailed on 17th escorted by *Arab* and *Norwich City*. We were unable to sail as our A/S gear was not repaired in time.

8.   We sailed a.m. on the 19th as escort to R.U.7 with *St. Keynon* (S.O.) *Vizalma* and 4 M/V's.

9.   The weather was bad and it took us 2 days to get clear of Reykjanes.

10.   On 22nd *St Keynon* ordered me to remain with the *Commodore* who was very slow (*Lysaker*) and he went ahead with the other ships.

11.   I lost touch with *Lysaker* a.m. on the 24th in heavy weather and proceeded alone.

12.   During the 24th a strong westerly gale took charge of us and we were obliged to run before it and chance going aground during the night. We tried to get D/F bearings from the naval stations without success but at 0600/25 got a bearing from Malin Head which solved the difficulty, and the sea also moderated.

> GRAEME OGDEN
> LIEUTENANT, R.N.V.R.

Captain (D)
Greenock 27 Jan 1942

That evening the wind and sea increased, and I became uneasy, as I knew the danger of being caught running, especially at night, when it is difficult to judge the size of the waves. Anyway, other events took charge, for we picked up an S O S from a ship called *Lyra II*, who gave her position a little to the west of us, so we turned back to look for her.

Turning a small ship in a big sea is risky and if you don't do it correctly you can quite easily lose your ship. The first thing to do is to study the size and length of the sea, and watch how it is running. In a big turbulent sea the waves are not regularly dispersed, and are not of the same size—you often get two whoppers in seven or one in three. I don't think there is any set rule about this, you just have to watch it. It is essential to remember that a small ship, to be safe, should imitate a seagull and ride up and down on the waves and not try to cut though them. The first part of a turn into the wind is getting beam to sea, which is all too easy, but the danger period is when you are in the trough, for if a big sea breaks over the ship you can't get out. The ship must be got into the trough in a lull and then given a short burst of full ahead, but not until full rudder—if you go hard over, and you have misjudged the situation, you may break your steering. Give her helm the way she wants to go. I always think handling a ship is very like riding a horse. You have got to be firm, but must take advantage of your ship's willingness to carry out a manœuvre. Once out of the trough, revert to 'operation seagull'—edge round slowly into the wind. A well-designed ship such as *Lady M* will do most of the work on her own, provided she isn't driven into a position she can't cope with.

We made the turn, but we never found *Lyra II*, though I heard afterwards that she staggered back to port. We were now in trouble, for instead of remaining head to wind and heaving to, deceived by the darkness and a slight lull in the storm, I turned east again. By midnight I realized I had made a serious mistake, for both sea and wind were higher and we had almost run the distance, that is to say, on my reckoning, we should be near the land. I knew my calculations were not accurate, because a Walker's trident log never runs true in a big following sea. By turning back I had confused the issue and lost my own bearings. I didn't know how much to allow for drift and had to watch the sea like a hawk, for if I went too fast the propeller raced, and put a dangerous strain on the ship's engines and steering gear.

The weather conditions were now so bad that I didn't think that even *Lady M* would turn away from the land; anyway, not without doing herself a lot of damage and risking getting her fires put out by a big sea going down the smoke-stack. To say I felt 'very uneasy' is an understatement. I was, in fact, obsessed with the ghastly fear that I had got my ship and her crew into a situation from where there was no escape. For the first time I was thoroughly frightened. I had done the one thing that I had always dreaded, and we were in a position where we could easily lose our ship and our lives—but not in the face of enemy action. Small ships quite often disappeared in Atlantic gales, and nobody knew their fate. To fight one's ship and die in battle was one thing, but to be 'lost at sea', for the reason that the captain didn't know his job, was an appalling thought.

I decided to call an emergency conference of my officers and senior hands, some of whom were more experienced than I was. In Donald I had probably the finest small-ship helmsman afloat, and Whitehead had known the sea since childhood. Besides Sloan, Glue, Blundell and Armstrong, many of the crew had been fishermen, born to the sea. Geoff, as his stocky figure and wild appearance proclaimed, was a born fighter; Bill Sedgewick, with his wide-set eyes, was cool and fearless; and Mac was at his best in dangerous situations. Apart from 'Their Lordships' grave displeasure', it was my love for these men and my ship that made my stomach turn over and my nerves ache. I seemed to be the weak link in this otherwise strong chain. In my bewilderment, I prayed to God to come to my aid...'Eternal Father, strong to save...'

We had the conference in my cabin, as there at least we could hear ourselves speak and the voice-pipe to the bridge was unavailable. As we assembled, our faces were drawn and hard, and we must have looked a strange and fearsome company—Whitehead, straight from the engine-room, with the inevitable sweat-rag round his neck, and the giant Sloan in oilskins. None of us wore naval uniform.

Looking back, I am sure that the hard core of the ship's personnel was forged in these frightening minutes. We were facing an ignominious death together, and if we survived nothing was ever going to break the faith we had in one another, or our personal friendship. The fact that we did survive made *Lady M*'s future adventures possible.

This was the beginning of what I think of as 'the highwire act'—acrobats on the tight-rope depending upon understanding, training and experience. In our case it was the Chief, Donald and myself who later on were able to avoid the shower of bombs aimed at us for days on end. We invented a language of our own—the chief could move his engines with an unbelievable accuracy and Donald could steer the ship round a sixpence. One mistake would have done us in, but it never happened—however, that part of this story comes later.

Now we decided to carry on. I still didn't feel at all secure, as the night was the wildest I had ever known at sea. Ugly black squalls tore down upon us, blotting out the stars and menacing our existence. Having told the chief to slow *Lady M* down as much as he dared, after assuring him I would see she didn't lose steerage way, I ordered the ship's company to stand by in their life-jackets and warned them that we might go aground at any minute. Look-outs were doubled, and I put on my own life-belt for the first time.

At 0600 the next morning we saw land on the port bow. Now came a vital decision. Should I turn north, or south, or go on? I had no idea what the land was; visibility was bad and it was still dark. I felt pretty sure we were to the south'ard, and so turned north. Immense seas were still running, but some of the spite had gone out of the wind; even so, we had a battle to make anything to the nor'ard. Half a mile to the east, we could see huge rollers crashing on to jagged rocks and flinging up fountains of spray. Later in the day we were able to identify the land as Malin Head, so, had I turned south or gone on the same course, we should have piled up on the rocks of the Irish Free State and been either drowned or interned for the duration of the war.

We limped back to Greenock, bleary-eyed and completely

flaked out. On our way we saw a huge ship aground on the Mull of Kintyre, and the air was thick with W/T messages asking for assistance. I believe about thirty ships went ashore in the Minches and St. George's Channel. A Norwegian I met later on told me that ten of their convoy went ashore, including the S.O. of the escort, who fetched up on the beach next to the Commodore!

We went alongside Albert Harbour, and D was there to meet us. The rest of the party had all got back earlier, but some alarmist had started the buzz that we were lost, so I think D was more than relieved to see us—we were certainly glad to see him. He told us that he'd had enough of having his ships messed about and that this time we were not going to sea again until we had refitted.

'Turn in and have a good rest,' said D. 'If anybody comes worrying you with bits of paper send 'em to me.' A week later I got a signal to say that *Lady M* and *Ayrshire* were to refit at Ardrossan, and thither we proceeded in company at the beginning of February 1942. It was bitterly cold, the dockyard was covered with snow and we found the town a depressing place. Like Gaul, a refit is divided into three parts: the defects, additions and alterations, and what really gets done. It is a three-cornered contest between the dockyard, the Admiralty overseer and the C.O. of the ship. The defect list is usually taken in hand without much fuss, but the alterations and additions are always a battle. The C.O. wants the moon, the dockyard say they can't do it and Admiralty say they won't pay for it. D had, however, said to me, 'When you refit, make your ship the best fighting unit you can, as you are going on Russian convoys.'

Leo went on leave (to see his red-and-white 'buoy'), and I sent Geoff off, as he had got up steam to propose to his girl friend. Dick Elsden, of *Ayrshire*, and I stayed behind to find 'the battle of Ardrossan'.

This time we were determined to get some of the equipment we needed so badly to make our ships efficient fighting units. The problem was how to get it. From all we heard from the dockyard, our prospects of getting what we wanted were non-existent. Dick

Elsden, who was responsible for *Ayrshire*, and I went into conference and decided upon a method of solving the difficulty.

We concocted a most impressive-looking signal, classified it as 'Confidential' so it would have to go out on pink paper (which is reserved for important signals), gave it a high degree of W/T priority and dispatched it to every dockyard concerned with our refit—and possibly quite a few that weren't!

The key phrase was, I remember, 'Admiralty approval having been granted, you are to dispatch forthwith...'

We then listed the items we wanted: whalers, refrigerators, guns, radar equipment, long-range W/T transmitters and receivers and various other longed-for accessories.

Our signal worked like a charm and within an incredibly short time the quay was stacked high with the most exciting-looking packing cases, plus two lovely new whalers. The one snag was that since Admiralty approval for our needs had not even been asked for it could hardly have been given, and this led to a certain amount of sourness among the suppliers and the local dockyard staff. However, Dick and I got the gear aboard our ships in record time and before officialdom had woken up we had apologized to our Captain D (whose disapproval was very superficial) and sailed away with our booty.

We heard later that 'The O.E. Plan' was used by other trawler captains when refitting their ships with considerable success.

I've heard doctors say, 'It's a case of having to be worse to get better,' but after the dockyard has been let loose on one's ship for two or three weeks, to all intents and purposes the patient has died. *Lady M* was on the operating table and I was fearful that she might not recover and I might never feel her heart begin to beat again.

Geoff came back, having got engaged, looking the same as usual, his corn-coloured hair untidy and his blue eyes full of merriment. Donald was around, having been on local leave and not to his native Aberdeen, so I enquired how the little lad was and got a full report. Squires packed me up with his usual efficiency. I was off to Liverpool, to the Western Approaches tactical course, and I was overcome when he volunteered to go with me 'to see I was properly looked after'.

On arriving at Liverpool I made my number at Western Approaches Command and found the place buzzing with activity. I was shown the operations room, where the staff officers kept track of all convoy movements on a vast wall chart of the North Atlantic. Reports of U-boat attacks, convoy losses and estimated U-boat positions were carefully marked up by luscious-looking Wrens wearing black silk stockings. When they mounted a ladder to alter the position of some far northern group a momentary hush fell over the Operations Room.

The man in charge of the C.O.'s tactical course was one Captain Roberts, R.N.R., and from the moment he began his first lecture I found him completely fascinating. A man of mystery, he was of striking appearance, and walked with a distinct limp. Where he got his information from I doubt if anybody will ever know. His genius was not always accepted in top R.N. circles; however, he had such a wealth of suggestion and knowledge at his command, plus the actor's personality to put it over, that he was the ideal man for the job. He inspired such respect in me that I can remember almost everything he told us.

His most important contribution was that the U-boat should not be considered as a 'submarine' at all, but as a surface raider, capable of submerging when hunted. He explained the method used by Doenitz's U-boat captains for locating our convoys, and their procedure of attacking them. Much to everybody's consternation, he told us that the regularity and accuracy of the U-boats' interception of our convoys was inexplicable—unless the Germans were reading our codes!

The course included technical subjects such as the performance of the VIIa 500-ton U-boat, which was the one we were at present up against. Our side, apparently, knew its surface and underwater speeds, its endurance and torpedo capacity, but we didn't know how deep it could dive. The maximum setting on our depth-charges was 500 ft. Captain Roberts suggested that, under stress, one of these U-boats could dive to nearly 1,000 ft. When I asked him how on earth anybody had determined that the standard speed at which a cylindrical depth-charge (weighing 4 cwt.) sank was 10 ft. per second, he smiled rather sadly, so I shut up. I would have liked to enquire why depth-charges were made in the shape of large tin cans and not stream-lined like bombs or shells. A thing like a large oil-drum thrown into a big sea couldn't possibly have a standard rate of fall.

At the torpedo lectures Captain Roberts brought us up to date with the latest German types, the magnetic and the new horror which homed on to its prey acoustically. He also told us that in the early stages of the war, especially in the Norwegian invasion, the Germans had had serious trouble with their magnetic pistol torpedo, but this had been corrected. They had, for some time, had to go back to their contact pistol.

I was so intrigued by Captain Roberts that one evening I succeeded in getting him to have dinner with me. He then told me the most surprising story of all. Apparently, Professor Walter— from Robert's description a German rather like the schoolmaster in *The Blue Angel*—had, before the war, invented an entirely different kind of submarine motor. His U-boat did not have to use diesel motors on the surface and electric motors when submerged, but had a propulsion unit which gave a U-boat a speed of over 20 knots on the surface, or when submerged. Roberts was terrified that this revolutionary type of U-boat might come into service. If it did, he affirmed, we had lost the battle of the Atlantic—and probably the war too.

He went on to explain that our Asdic instruments could never cope with an underwater craft with such a speed. After hearing this, although we had eaten and drunk the best the Adelphi Hotel could provide, I took my leave feeling rather sick in the stomach. 'The crafty old Hun,' I thought to myself, 'is always cooking up some ghastly new horrors.' In the last war it had been Zeppelins, poison gas and 'Big Bertha'. So far, this time, we had been subjected to the dive-bomber and the magnetic mine. I wondered what else we were in for; not, I hoped, a super U-boat. It seemed strange, all the same, that the existing 500-ton German submarines differed very little from their predecessor of the 1914-18 war.

A fter the course ended I had a few days' leave, so I made for London, hoping to meet Sally before her evening show, but failed dismally, as Liverpool had an air-raid that night and I didn't reach my destination until noon the next day. Sally was out, so I spent the time buying flowers, visiting the Bond Street milliners, gazing into Cartier's window and trying to remember all the things I had planned to say to her.

One of the things I wanted most was for Sally to 'adopt' Lady M. Most ships had distinguished patrons, whose duty it was to take an interest in the ship's company and provide them with some of the things we were all so sorely in need of, such as warm clothing, books, magazines and food. This was all very well, but what price a rusty old trawler manned by an odd lot of amateurs and fishermen?

Long before my leave was over I got my wish, and Sally agreed to become the 'chatelaine' of Lady Madeleine. We collected some startlingly lovely photographs of her, to be distributed to the various messes, and one very special one for me. This, I need hardly say, was always with me wherever we went. As we shall see, Sally turned out to be a wonderful 'Fairy Godmother' to Lady M. We got all sorts of presents in the most unexpected places—such as Murmansk— and my stock shot up with the ship's company. I thought of her as Wendy looking after the lost boys in the never-never-land.

The days went by too quickly. The band at The 400 knew our

favourite tunes, and the head waiter at The Aperitif in Jermyn Street knew what we liked to eat. There were wonderful things to remember. The black hat she always wore, which, with its heavy gold ornaments, looked like something between an Egyptian head-dress and a Foreign Légionnaire's helmet. The brave goodbye, with Miss Carlton outwardly composed and the commanding officer of H.M.S. *Lady Madeleine* trying to keep the tears out of his eyes.

As the train from Euston rattled northwards, I could still see Sally's face and smell her perfume. The rhythm of the train wheels played our favourite tunes.

We had exchanged our identity bracelets. It was wonderful to see the slim gold chain of her bracelet round my own wrist and to think of her wearing mine. I wondered what would happen if death or disaster should come to either of us. It would have confused the world in general if Sally had been reported 'lost in North Russia', or if I had been officially blown up in a London air-raid.

On returning to Ardrossan I found *Lady M* still a shambles. In the dry dock she looked so naked that it seemed rather embarrassing for both of us. So far we had steamed more than twice round the world together, possibly sunk a U-boat, attacked many more and rescued some hundred sailors from a watery grave. We had also taken a part in convoying some thousand merchant ships, comparatively few of which had been sunk, although S.C.108 had been a disaster. We had been so overworked that there had been no time to think about our lives outside our duties as an escort ship. Now, for the first time in a year or more, I was able to think back and take stock of what had happened to me. In summer there had been unforgettably beautiful days when we had sailed beneath great wheeling Atlantic skies, days when our companions were huge cathedrals of white clouds drifting on to eternity. Nights pierced with hard, bright stars and moons which turned the sea to silver. One had learnt to sleep accompanied by the sound of the waves as they slapped against the ship's sides. In bright sunlight one watched the ship's stern cutting through the indigo water and turning it into snow. Never did I tire of watching the greens and blues of the ocean swell merge into the colours of the sunset and the dawn, but always, when the light began to fade, one felt a creepy-crawly feeling coming on because, when the day had gone, the night meant peril from the U-boats. I wondered what the Arctic would be like. Would I see the aurora borealis and the midnight sun? Would I be able to bring home some Russian furs for Sally?

As I write there seems a lot to remember about those days in the Atlantic.

For instance, once I nearly became an American millionaire! This happened when we were making passage on our own from Greenland to the Clyde. We had been detached from a convoy to go to a ship in distress, who gave her position as off Cape Farewell. We never found this ship, if it ever existed, but going home in good weather we came across a large American freighter which had been torpedoed amidships and was sinking on an even keel. From our point of view, the rescue of the crew was easy, but from their point of view if we hadn't turned up they would have had a long row home and so they were very pleased with us. I gave the skipper the run of my day cabin, which was under the wheelhouse, and told him to help himself to a drink. Some hours later I came down off the bridge to see how he was getting on, and found my large chart table weighed down with bundles of neatly stacked 100-dollar bills. He greeted me profusely and assured me I had saved his life and those of his crew. This didn't impress me, because we were constantly rescuing ships' crews, but this American had taken the matter very much to heart. He told me that he had been the last to leave his sinking ship, one of the U.S. pay vessels, and had found time to go to the ship's safe, so he had come aboard with four heavy suitcases. They contained, he told me, about half a million dollars—now on my chart table. When I got over my surprise, he told me that nobody would ever know if he had been to his ship's safe before she sank or not. With a gesture I shall never forget, he 'cut the pack in half', saying, 'Thanks, Bud, for saving our lives, we split even.' Mug that I am, I refused the offer, but put him, his suitcases and his crew ashore off Ireland in their two or three very excellent life-boats we had towed for some 900 miles. I wonder what was the end of the episode.

Then there was the incident of a new *Marie Celeste*. One night, after a heavy U-boat attack, we were miles astern of the convoy, looking for stragglers. We stooged about for hours, but could find no ships. This, I must tell you, was a fast convoy and it took us days to catch up. On the first day, when we were alone in the ocean in fine weather, nothing happened, but the following night I saw a pink smudge in the darkness. We closed and discovered a deserted 5,000-ton Norwegian freighter. She had been on fire, and her plates were still glowing, and I made the mistake of getting too near and 'singeing *Lady M*'s hair'. I made the appropriate signals and stood by. About twenty-four hours later I was able to get a boarding party away, and they returned to tell me a most fantastic story. Apparently the fire had been in her holds and the bridge and officers' quarters were hardly damaged, but the life-boats had been launched and there was no sign of any living soul. I was so interested I went aboard myself—it was the most uncanny experience. When the ship had cooled off there was little the matter with her. As salvage she was ours, if we could tow her back to port. Even in wartime you get 10 per cent of the value of a derelict ship if it is deserted and you tow it back to a port. Well, we weren't in the war for money, but a share-out of, say, £100,000 for *Lady M*'s crew was not to be sniffed at. We decided to have a go. This is really rather a sad story, because 200 miles off Ireland it started to blow. I had to put some of *Lady M*'s crew aboard the other ship and they couldn't handle her and keep the tow-line intact, so I was forced to take them off and send for salvage tugs. These duly arrived and took over from us, but I often wonder what happened to this ship and her crew. We did at least live for months on excellent canned food and schnapps, and I acquired the best sextant I have ever had.

One could go on thinking about those days for ages. When the battle of the Atlantic was at its height you lived in a series of alarms, depth-charge explosions and stricken ships. My feelings at the time were: There is no doubt that U-boats are the devil, but they are clearly manned by brave determined crews. If I survive this contest, one day I should like to talk to a U-boat commander and learn his side of the picture. It's very difficult to say now who is going to win the battle at sea, but the man on the surface is bound to wonder what goes through the mind of his adversary below. We are fighting each other now, but I have a feeling of admiration for the U-boat C.O.s and their crews. Either they will perish or we will—it's as simple as that. Professor Walter's new-type boat could be the winning factor.

But to return to Ardrossan dockyard. Leo was back and in difficulties with *Ayrshire*, so we fought the dockyard authorities during the day and retired to the local in the evenings.

We each had a skeleton crew aboard, forming a care-and-maintenance party, so we combined forces and got up a dart match against the local army team. I offered to stand the beer and as the Navy won I felt very happy until the landlord gave me a bill for over a fiver.

We were living ashore, and next morning, when Leo didn't put in an appearance at breakfast, I went to his room to see how he was getting on. I saw a very strange sight indeed: the room looked as if there had been a heavy fall of snow; Leo was sound asleep, apparently buried in snowflakes. I couldn't make it out at all. One further investigation I discovered that the distinguished counsel had gone to sleep with a cigarette in his mouth, which had ignited his pillow. This, obviously, had necessitated some midnight firefighting and, having dealt with the emergency, Leo had gone to sleep again amidst a cloud of feathers.

A ship really never finishes refitting. What happens is that there comes a time when all the main items have been done, the dockyard want to get on with another job, the Admiralty overseer has already spent too much money and the C.O. is pining to get back to his ship and get her out of the dockyard.

After a very good refit, although it had been a hard fight, I took *Lady M* away from Ardossan in early April. I had asked for Oerlikon guns and R.D.F., much to everybody's amusement. Oerlikons on a trawler—what next! However, my letter to Captain D had borne fruit and I got part of my wish.

I took the ship back to Greenock, and there was told we were to be based in Iceland and sail from there on North Russian convoys. I was sorry to leave Greenock, D, and the 'Fighting 49th', but excited that we were going to Russia.

I was tired of the Atlantic and keen to try the Arctic. *Rari nantes in gurgite vasto!*

BOOK TWO

DANGER IN THE SUN

B efore we left the Clyde there was a great deal to be done. *Lady M* had to do her steaming and gunnery trials, and be fully stored and ammunitioned, special charges, codes and Arctic equipment had to be collected, and our water-tanks and coal-bunkers topped up to the brim.

After our last farewell to Captain D and our friends at Greenock, we sailed for Hvalfiord.

At Ardrossan we had gone in for a new type of camouflage. The colour scheme was white, with light-blue and green triangles. By far the largest proportion was white, so we really looked very like a yacht, but, as we shall see, this nearly proved our undoing.

We left home behind us; we knew we should not be returning for many months—if at all—for we were going on 'The Northern Crusade'. I only hoped that ours would not be as disastrous as its medieval predecessors, which had left disease, death and ruin in their train.

The weather was fine and we took the opportunity to test our new equipment and carry out exercises.

Rather nostalgically, we heard Vera Lynn's voice get fainter and fainter as she sang, over the B.B.C. Home programme, 'Somewhere over the Rainbow' and 'The White Cliffs of Dover'. 'Sparks' could tell to a few miles how far away from the coast we were when 'we lost Vera' (in good weather about 230 miles, a fact which I don't doubt the U-boats were very grateful for).

When we anchored at Hvalfiord on 10th May we found the fiord full of shipping and a scene of great naval activity. A Home Fleet base, under whose orders we now were, had been set up and already fifteen convoys had sailed northwards to Russia. These convoys were labelled P.Q. on the outward trip and Q.P. on the homeward one. On reporting to base, I discovered that the state of the game was that P.Q.15 had sailed at the end of April, and that we were going on P.Q.16, which was due to sail in about ten days' time. The commanding officer of the close escort was to be Captain R.G. Onslow in *Ashanti*, and *Lady M* was now under his orders.

I duly made my number with Onslow, who turned out to be a most charming person—tall, elegant and well dressed, I felt he would be more at home in White's, in St. James's Street, than the Arctic. How wrong I was!

In any small isolated community news travels fast, the more secret it is the faster it travels, and we soon learnt that P.Q.15 had run into serious trouble. The Icelandic air was buzzing with rumours.

We heard that the Commodore had lost his ship, that an ammunition ship had blown up with a terrific explosion killing all hands and that the Germans were now using torpedo-bombers as well as U-boats and dive-bombers. Worse still, there had been a battle between our escorts and some German destroyers, in which we had lost the cruiser *Edinburgh* and possibly also the *Trinidad*. Our destroyers had also taken a beating; somebody even went as far as to say one of our battleships on the distant covering screen had rammed one of our own destroyers!

Geoff and I were inclined to brush off these ugly rumours, but a few days later, when we took *Lady M* round to Recky, we saw a sight which told its own sad tale. Across our bows steamed two F-class destroyers. These ships were near wrecks: their masts were down, their sides holed, their smoke-stacks askew, they bore the scars of German shells and their own gun-turrets were a shambles. It was a gallant sight to watch these ships, with their battle ensigns still on the yardarm, steam into harbour, but it was a grim reminder of what might be in store for us. We returned to Hvalfiord, having been inspected by A.C.I.C., in rather a chastened mood.

The convoy conference for P.Q.16 was summoned for 20th May and I went with Graham Butcher, the C.O. of *St. Elstan*, who was a friend of mine. We felt very insignificant as R.N.R. and R.N.V.R. lieutenants amidst the distinguished company we found ourselves in. The conference room was congested with R.N. officers in brass hats and uniforms lavishly decorated with gold lace and medals.

Our virgin chests were rather conspicuous. This was like a visit to the Royal Opera House by members of the Greenock Repertory Company. We took two back seats and sat down to listen. The stage-setting was the familiar one.

The first person on the stage was N.S.C.O., who really should be regarded as 'the producer'. He talked about the routing, the weather, the charts, the convoy's rendezvous with its main escorts and so on. The first actor—we may as well regard this conference as a tragedy in which we were among the chorus—was Admiral Sir Harold Burrough, who was in charge of the operation. He is a man of great personal distinction and radiates confidence—after the adventures of P.Q.15 we needed it. In the traditional bluff naval style he assured us all that we had little to fear, as the escort for this convoy was the most powerful ever to be sent on a north Russian convoy. He, with four cruisers, would be near us all the way up, and battleships would be covering the convoy as a distant screen.

We listened respectfully and felt somewhat relieved. It was now youth's turn in the shape of Captain R.G. Onslow (complete with monocle) and, as commanding officer of the close escort, he more than anybody else was responsible for the convoy's safety. He carefully went over the sailing instructions we had all been issued, and made as certain as he could that the merchant captains understood them. This wasn't too easy, as they were a mixed lot of various nationalities. The chorus, however, made the right noises at the appropriate moments and the conference suddenly disintegrated.

Butcher and I, grasping sheaves of papers, then went aboard H.M.S. *Ashanti* for the escort conference. Here Captain Onslow really got down to business and had the whole situation at his finger-tips. He told us what we could expect from the enemy and discussed his general conception of convoy formations, emergency measures under attack, distress signals, communication arrangements, the route along the edge of the ice fields, the position in the convoy of the Commodore, the A.A. ship and the catapult ship and the two submarines which were going with us. I was most impressed with this man's efficiency. The conference ended with drinks in the wardroom, where Onslow bade us good luck.

Back in *Lady M*, Geoff and I sat down to study the pile of papers I had brought back with me. From what we could make out at first glance P.Q.16 was a 10-knot convoy consisting of thirty-five merchant ships. Its Commodore was Captain N.H. Gale in the *Ocean Voice*. The escort was truly impressive, for the cruiser squadron, under the command of Admiral Burrough, who flew his flag in *Nigeria*, included the *Liverpool, Norfolk* and *Kent*, together with the fleet destroyers *Onslow, Oribi* and *Marne*. This force was to join us off Jan Mayen Island.

The close escort under Onslow was made up of the destroyers *Ashanti, Martin, Achates, Volunteer* and *Garland* (Polish), the corvettes *Honeysuckle, Starwort, Hyderabad* and *Roselys* (French), the trawlers *St. Elstan, Northern Spray, Retriever* and *Lady Madeleine*, plus the A.A. ship *Alynbank* and the minesweeper *Hazard*. Two fleet oilers were to sail with the convoy and so were two of our submarines. When fully assembled Geoff and I made the convoy and its close escort sixty-one ships in all.

Here was an armada—I hoped it would be more successful than the one which sailed on a northerly course from Cadiz.

The time-table was that the merchant ships were to sail from the anchorage at Hvalfiord with a small escort, of which we were to be part, on 21st May at 1100.

The destroyer escorts from Seydisfjörd were to join on the 22nd and the cruisers two days later.

The convoy was routed to pass east of Jan Mayen Island, then northward, leaving Bear Island to starboard, should this be possible. However, since in the spring the drifting ice barrier comes further south, this is problematical. The idea was to keep close to the ice edge, thus putting as great a distance as possible between the convoy and the German-occupied Norwegian coast.

Once past Bear Island—which for some strange reason is also known as Cherry Tree Island—we were to make a broad easterly arc to the Kola inlet and so to Murmansk and Archangel.

When Geoff and I had finished studying the convoy sailing orders and instructions I sent for Mac and Bill and gave them a résumé of the situation. The three divisional officers then departed to make a final check-up of their responsibilities.

It really seemed rather absurd, for as everybody in the ship knew exactly where we were going it was hardly necessary to tell them, but as the convoy's destination was supposed to be 'Most Secret', I cleared lower deck in the dog watch and addressed the ship's company. There were the familiar faces of Whitehead the chief, the second engineer, Turner, Sloan, Donald, Blundell, Glue, Geordie, Gaunt, Haliday, Bunts, Squires, Uncle Tom Cobbleigh and all.

I started on what I considered to be a suitable harangue, and was just getting on to the subject of 'what a great honour it was for the ship to be chosen for such a vital mission etc.', when one of the stokers standing near me let out a terrible oath *'sotto voce'* which could have been heard a mile away. The rest of my speech dried up in my mouth, so I gave up my script and told them in their own language what we were in for and what I expected of them. I made it clear that their best chance of survival was instant obedience to my orders, whatever might befall us, and that I would not have any nonsense from anybody.

That evening we had a sing-song, which was much more successful than my official speech, and when it was over I retired to my cabin to take stock of things. I gazed at Sally's photographs, patted the silver shoe and stowed away my No.1 uniform. I thought about saying my prayers, as I usually did, but tonight the words would not come. At the back of my mind I knew there must be millions of Germans praying to the same God and asking for victory, so I decided to read Belloc's *Cautionary Verses* instead. I read as far as:

'Young Algernon, the doctor's son
Was playing with a loaded gun.
He pointed it towards his sister
Aimed very carefully, but missed her...'

but my bunk looked so inviting that I turned in, as I was pretty sure this was going to be the last night I was going to have in it for the next ten days.

E arly next morning—which was Thursday, 21st May 1942—
the fiord was the centre of much activity. Steam winches
were being operated on the fo'c'sle of the merchant ships, and the
clanking of chains broke the early-morning silence as the anchor
cables rattled up the hawse pipes. Drifters hurrying about on last-
minute errands puffed up clouds of steam into the crisp air. Boilers
were being flashed up in the big ships and smoke spiralled lazily
skywards from forty funnels.

Below the Blue Peter, on the yardarm of the Commodore's
ship, fluttered the bright flags of a signal hoist and the other
merchantmen ran up their red-and-white answering pennants.
The sun was up and reflected in the ice-blue waters of the fiord.
Sea-birds swarmed and wheeled about the sterns of the ships,
taking their last tasty meal, and at exactly 1000 local time
Commodore Gale in the *Ocean Voice* blew a long blast on his ship's
siren and P.Q.16 was under way.

I noted the time of our departure in the deck-log and wrote:

P.Q.16 sailed from Hvalfiord at 1000 21.5.42. Course 290° speed 10 knots. Escorts H.M.S. *Hazard, Northern Wave, Retriever, Lady Madeleine, St. Elstan.* Weather fine, wind light airs—visibility good—log zero—barometer 29·8. Convoy's destination—Murmansk—distance approximately 2,500 miles. Estimated time of arrival Saturday 30.5.42.

Outside the fiord the convoy formed up into two long columns and steamed north-westwards on a course of 290 degrees; our position was on the port quarter. Geoff had the forenoon watch, but I said I would take over so that he could have a last-minute check-up round the ship. I did this because I wanted, while I had time, to try out once again the new action stations we had agreed on. The ship's company were accustomed to going to anti-submarine action stations from our Atlantic days, but there had been very few air attacks. For this trip we had worked out 'combined action stations', as the convoy would probably be attacked by U-boats and aircraft simultaneously. The standard signal on the alarm gongs was a series of 'shorts' for A.A. and a series of 'longs' for A/S, but as we were going to use only one signal for this trip—a series of long short longs.

Under the new drill we wore tin hats and life-belts and our positions were as follows:

No.1 was responsible for the part of the ship for'ard of the bridge, and was to shelter under the steel whaleback in air attacks to preserve himself to take command if anything happened to me up on the bridge.

No.2 was to control the 4 in. and for'ard machine guns.

No.3 was aft with the twin Vickers A.A. gun and was also in charge of the depth-charge party.

Mallard, the second engineer, was to handle the damage-control party, and Whitehead, the chief engineer, was to remain at the controls and make sure the watertight bulkheads were closed.

Turner was to be in the wheelhouse below me, with Donald on the wheel.

The leading signalman, a messenger and myself were stationed on the open top bridge and the two asdic ratings in the A/S cabin behind.

Goodness knows, we had practised this routine often enough, but I thought I would try in actual convoy conditions, so without any warning I put on my tin hat and life-belt and pressed the alarm.

The crew turned out in record time, but I am sorry to say not according to plan. Hardly anyone had on their tin hats and life-belts, Geoff went to the 4 in. and on finding Mac there rushed hatless on the upper bridge, Turner the coxswain took over the wheel as Donald had failed to appear, the second engineer went to the wardroom (he was supposed to assemble his part in the seamen's mess), and to put the lid on it, Squires suddenly appeared on the bridge with the ship's cat in his arms! I spent the next hour sorting out the situation.

At 2000 that evening the convoy altered course to 017 degrees, and at 0600 the next morning to 052 degrees. At noon on Friday 22nd I wrote in the log:

Position 66°50′ North, 22° West, speed 10 knots, course 074° wind force 3—visibility good—Log reading 248 miles. Barometer steady. Crossed 100 fathom line at 1130.

So the first twenty-four hours had been uneventful. I was relieved about that for we were now off the north-west cape of Iceland in the Denmark Strait. The actual distance to Greenland is about180 miles, but the ice edge is an unknown quantity in May, probably narrowing the passage to a little over a hundred miles of open water.

As we were well within range of U-boats and P.Q.16 was only protected by our escort, I was surprised we had not been attacked before the powerful destroyer escort joined us on the morrow. Thirty-five ships in two columns stretched for five miles in an ideal U-boat target, so in spite of all the hullabaloo at Hvalfiord I could only think that so far the Germans were unaware the convoy had sailed, or, knowing our route and destination, weren't bothering at this stage of the game. We managed to get some sleep that night, which was wonderful. At 0900 on Saturday, 23rd May, Captain Onslow in *Ashanti*, with the other destroyers, leaving the slower flower-class corvettes behind him, approached the convoy at speed. On a fine sparkling day, five destroyers tearing along at 30 knots is a gallant sight to see, and Onslow was enough of a showman to steam right round the convoy to make sure his arrival had been noticed by all the merchantmen. He immediately took over control of P.Q.16 and spent the next five hours in getting the convoy into a broad front of eight columns of approximately four ships deep. This formation was designed to make it more difficult for dive bombers to attack from astern, their favourite manœuvre.

At noon I wrote in the log:

Position 67°40′. 13°15′W. Destroyer escort from Seidisfiord joined 0900 hrs. Convoy reforming into broad front—new course 40°—speed 10 knots—weather fine—log reads 502 miles, barometer steady. H.M.T. *Retriever* left for Iceland.

I have never gathered why *Retriever* went home at this time, and can only suppose she had engine trouble or some severe mechanical defect. There were now three trawlers.

Early next morning, which was Sunday, 24th May, a German reconnaissance plane appeared over the horizon and began to circle methodically round the convoy. It flew at about 1,000 ft. and kept well out of range of the escort's guns.

I realized, with a sickening feeling, that this solitary enemy aircraft was the messenger of death and disaster for P.Q.16. From now onwards the convoy's fate would be held in the retina of a

German pilot's eye. Its struggle to avoid destruction by twisting and turning would now be of no avail. There could be no escape. The barbed harpoon had been plunged into the whale's side, not to be withdrawn until its captors had killed it and its blood had turned the pale Arctic sea to crimson. As I watched this evil shadow through my glasses, I thought of it as a gigantic bat, a *Fledermaus*, a spectre consorting with a butcher, a *Schlachter*. I knew for certain that P.Q.16 was under sentence of death; it was now only a question of how many of our ships and their crews were going to perish in the icy waters of the Arctic seas. I wondered what the fate of *Lady M* and *her* crew was going to be. Was her judge, either in heaven or on earth, about to don his black cap, or was he going to remit her sentence? I knew I was about to attend a funeral—but was it going to be my own?

We were plagued with these sinister shads for the rest of the voyage northwards. Their function was to keep the German shore bases accurately informed about the convoy; giving its formation, position, course and speed, and the disposition and strength of the escort. These long-range aircraft, which relieved one another every four hours, also acted as a homing W/T beacon to the attacking enemy aircraft and submarines.

There was no darkness in which to hide in those northern latitudes and we were under observation by our executioners for twenty-four hours a day. On this occasion the Schlachters were in no hurry to kill their meat, so no attack developed that day. We wondered if the Germans were waiting for the cruisers—which they must have seen by now—to join the convoy, in order to have a concentrated target of warships and merchantmen, or were they not going to risk the danger of the cruiser's powerful A.A. guns? They knew we had no air cover and probably also that our one catapult Hurricane fighter aboard the S.S. *Empire Lawrence* wasn't very lethal as far as they were concerned. On this day *Lady M*'s log read:

Noon position 70°20′N. 8°11′W. Speed 10 knots. Course 65°.

Jan Mayen Island bears 340°, 20 miles—weather fine—logs reading 762 miles—German reconnaissance plane arrived.

Monday, 25th May, was *Lady M*'s birthday, and a very lively one it turned out to be. At 0600 Admiral Burrough's cruisers hove in sight, hull down, approaching us from the south-east. Although one has seen it time and again, the sight of large ships apparently cut in half by the curvature of the earth is a strange one. In this instance the visibility was so good that it accentuated this phenomenon.

In half an hour the *Nigeria, Liverpool, Kent* and *Norfolk*—the last two being of the 10,000-ton, three-funnel vintage, county class—joined P.Q.16 with their destroyer escort, making seven warships in all. The cruisers, tucked into the convoy lanes between the merchant ships, made a gallant and reassuring sight. The observers in the shad would have immediately reported the arrival of our cruisers to their bomber base in Norway, some 400 miles away to the east, so now we had to wait, anxiously scanning the empty sky with our binoculars, trying to guess what the enemy strategy would be. Just before noon we heard over our loudspeaker system:

AIR RAID WARNING. RED. ENEMY PLANES
APPROACHING GREEN 120° 15 MILES

We went to action stations—this time in good order—just in time to see far away to starboard some specks high up in the clear blue sky. At a guess I put their height at 15,000 ft. As the skein of J.U.88s approached P.Q.16 from astern, the three leading aircraft peeled off into a steep dive and, with engines screaming, hurtled down at 250 m.p.h. on to the convoy. They let go their bombs at about 3,000 ft., then, pulling out, flew down to sea-level before reforming and climbing back for another assault.

The first three attackers were greeted with an all-out barrage from the convoy's massed A.A. guns and it seemed impossible they could survive. The sky above the convoy was thick with black-and-yellow smoke patches. The noise of gun-fire shattered the Arctic stillness we had grown accustomed to and drowned the whine of the descending dive-bombers.

The first six bombs were well aimed, but fell amongst the convoy without scoring a direct hit. The three J.U.88s were undamaged, incredible though it seemed. The explanation was that the course of a dive-bomber is a parabola and not a straight line (the same thing is true of a bomb's flight), and at this period naval A.A. guns were sighted on the straight-line theory.

The attack continued and I counted twelve German bombers. Every time a trio of planes dived the escort's guns spat a hail of lead and high explosive at them. I saw one plane smash into the sea ahead of us like a gannet diving for food. After half an hour the J.U.88s retired, having scored a hit on the S.S. *Carlton* (not a good omen). The freighter, however, did not sink and *Northern Spray* was detached from the convoy to escort her back home. This left two trawlers, *St. Elstan* and *Lady M*. We secured from action stations and had some food. As a curtain-raiser, the morning's performance had not been too bad at all. All we knew was that the battle for P.Q.16 had now been joined.

In the afternoon smoke was visible to port and a little later on Q.P.12, the returning empty ships of P.Q.15, hove in sight. That meant that over a hundred ships must be concentrated in an area of some fifty square miles. I wondered if this was the moment the Luftwaffe had been waiting for.

Curiously enough, no attack developed until 1840 that evening, when Q.P.12 was well astern of us. The second attack was on the same lines as the first, but the pilots were not so bold and did not press home the attack, so no damage was done to either side.

After we had secured, Geoff came up on to the bridge to join me in a cigarette and discuss the situation so far; but our respite was short-lived, for now the alarm went out to stand by for U-boat attacks, so back we went to action stations. H.M.S. *Martin* had apparently sighted a U-boat on the surface and gone off to chase it and put it down. But, as I had learned from Captain Roberts, one U-boat means a concentration of U-boats within a short space of time. Admiral Doenitz must have been rubbing his hands in glee.

I wrote in the log:

Monday May 25th. Noon position 71º19′N. on Greenwich meridian 0º (so near and yet so far from home). Speed 10 knots. Course 65º—visibility 100%—wind force 4. Cruisers joined at 0600 hrs. First air attacks developed 1200 hrs. S.S. *Carlton* disabled—help!

During the next ten hours the German bombers ran a series of 'tip and run' raids with surprisingly little effect. The close escort and the cruisers blasted away at these shy birds, using up precious ammunition and scoring no hits.

At dawn next day the first wave of Heinkel III torpedo-bombers flitted like moths above the pale sea far away to port. This meant an attack was being mounted from this quarter, and we were between these planes and the convoy. We saw them first and gave the alarm. As they started their run in, I turned *Lady M* towards them and we let go with shrapnel shells from our 4 in. gun. The other escort on our side of the convoy did the same. The cruisers, hemmed in between the convoy lanes, couldn't fire their low-angle guns. The Heinkel pilots never pressed home this attack for some inexplicable reason, even though they had the cruisers at their mercy. Their torpedoes splashed into the water some 2,000 yards away and never found their mark. I never saw one running near *Lady M* and can only suppose they were set too deep and passed under the convoy.

At 0800 the cruisers pulled out of the convoy's ranks and left with their destroyer escort to cover P.Q.16 from German surface-raiders by steaming a parallel course between us and Norway. Although we were going to miss their fire power, I was glad to see them steam off intact. Their stay with the convoy had been a risky one. However, the shad had reported their withdrawal and within two hours the dive-bombers were back in force. This time there was nothing half-hearted about their attacks, and we felt the first eleven had turned out against us. The attack plan was of a difficult pattern, the bombers diving out of the sun and being supported by high-level bombers and low-flying torpedo-bombers. The attacks came from all points of the compass.

The rain of bombs churned up the sea into a multitude of water-spouts. The bombers were now arriving over the convoy in an unending stream, and attacked both the merchantmen and the escorts. The weather was still clear and one could see the pair of bombs leave the belly of a diving plane. If they were directed at your ship you had to judge the accuracy of the aim and either move the ship instantly or stay where you were—always remembering the parabola theory. *Lady M*'s 'tight-rope-walking' team were in action all day.

Soon the convoy was in distress. Two ships were blazing astern, others were stopped or sinking, and Onslow in *Ashanti* and Thompson in *Martin* dashed hectically to wherever the attack was the hottest. Commodore Gale in the *Ocean Voice* steamed with the main body of ships, and the rest of the escort tried to ward off the air attacks and give assistance to the damaged and burning ships. A little later on, two bombs detonated just above 'A' turret on the Polish destroyer *Garland*, who was just inside us on the starboard hand. I thought that it was a direct hit and went over to her. Both 'A' and 'B' turrets were on fire; volumes of black smoke were surging from her foredeck and she appeared to be burning fiercely. I took *Lady M* close to her and steamed a parallel course, flashing her to ask if she wanted any assistance. She sent back a message to say she was carrying on, and continued firing with her aft guns. It was thrilling.

I hung on, as I didn't believe they could get the fire under control, and later she asked us to go back and try to find some of her crew who had been blown overboard. We went back astern of the convoy and searched, and, although we could not find any of her sailors, we saw some remarkable sights. A burning ship had been abandoned in a hurry and been left with the engines running; *St. Elstan,* who was standing by another maimed ship taking off survivors, nearly got run down by this blazing rogue-elephant. An abandoned ship under steam was a menace and she had to be sunk by gun-fire.

Then there was the *Stari Bolshevik*, the Russian oiler, which was a mass of flames, amid dense columns of black smoke. She was so hot that *Rosalys* could not get near enough to pump water on to her, but the incredible thing is that those Russians fought that fire for days and refused to abandon their ship. More incredible still is that they eventually mastered the fire and brought their ship to Murmansk. I wrote at the time: 'This is a fine example of the heroism of the Russians. If sheer guts is any criterion, they should stop the German invasion of their country.'

New waves of dive-bombers (the experts) kept arriving, and more of our ships were blasted, maimed or sunk. In the middle of this battle the Cam ship, the S.S. *Empire Lawrence*, fired her one and only Hurricane off her foredeck by means of a rocket charge. It looked like some legendary dragon spitting out a gnat in a sheet of orange flame.

The pilot survived this ordeal and went tearing off at the nearest enemy plane. This he shot down amid cheers from the convoy. Then the most foul thing happened. The Hurricane flew back over the convoy, I suppose with the idea of showing his position prior to baling out, as by then he had run out of ammunition and had to ditch himself anyway. The gunners in the merchant ships were in such a state of jitters that they opened up at him and shot him down. When I saw what was happening I literally tore out my hair. By the grace of God the pilot was rescued by H.M.S. *Volunteer* and, although severely wounded, survived. He certainly deserved to live, and I hope he got a decoration too.

At 1420 the *Empire Lawrence* was hit and pulled out of her place in the convoy. I could not see how badly damaged she was, so I took *Lady M* over to her to help take off her crew if necessary. When I was nearly alongside, I noticed that her port-side life-boats were hanging vertically down the side of the ship, so I yelled to her captain and asked if he wanted my boats in the water. He shouted back something which I shall never know, for at that moment Geoff and I heard the cruel whine of bombers, and, looking aft, saw three of them diving on us. I heard the swish of falling bombs, but couldn't move our ship. The next thing I remember is that Geoff and I were rolling about on our backs on the deck of the A/S bridge and the sky was full of strange shapes. We were covered with falling wreckage and enveloped in suffocating brown smoke. I thought we had been hit. When, minutes later, the smoke cleared away, there was no sign of the 12,000-ton *Empire Lawrence*. The first thing I did was to light my pipe—I wanted to know if I was still alive. An oily pool—fringed with wreckage and bodies—and the shattered remains of a life-boat were all that remained of the *Empire Lawrence*. *Lady M* was untouched, although we were lying with our engines stopped, the length of a cricket pitch away.

We heard afterwards from *Hazard*, who was just astern of us, that when they saw *Lady M* emerge from the smoke cloud, her gay camouflage bright in the sunshine, they could hardly believe it.

Onslow in *Ashanti* thought we were gone, for he signalled incredulously: 'Do you need assistance?'

I answered: '*Empire Lawrence* sunk, am picking up survivors.'

We had but a few yards to move to pick up the survivors. Some were terribly wounded, and our own lads jumped over the side to help get them inboard. Fortunately, trawlers have little freeboard, especially in the waist, and, the sea being like a millpond, I was able to manœuvre *Lady M* alongside the badly wounded, who were unable to move, and get them aboard. Our sea-boats collected the others. Sixteen in all, including the radar officer, who was apparently unharmed.

We agreed afterwards, when making out the report of the loss of the *Empire Lawrence*, that of the six bombs aimed at her at least three must have been direct vertical hits and that they knocked the bottom out of her. She had sunk in a matter of seconds.

Bill Sedgewick, in charge of our first-aid party, gave the wounded morphia and took care of the others the best he could. I sent Geoff to look round the ship to see if we had got damaged, Mac took the opportunity of getting up more ammunition and I set *Lady M* off at full speed to rejoin the convoy. The engine-room, fortunately, didn't know how close they had been to death, so I gave the chief a toned-down report over the voice-pipe.

It was now 1700 and we were miles astern of the convoy. We secured from action stations and took a hasty meal. We had been closed up for about eight hours. When I say a meal, we didn't go below to eat, but sat down near our action stations drinking cocoa and munching cold bully-beef with ship's biscuits. We also had 'up spirits' to celebrate *Lady M*'s survival. Squires in a fur cap, looking like Robinson Crusoe, was in his element and, apart from his rig, behaved like the family butler at a point-to-point. After this he became known as 'my man Friday'.

An hour later I found *Martin* astern of the convoy and closed her. As we didn't carry a doctor or even a sick-bay attendant, I asked Thompson if I could go alongside him and transfer the worst of the wounded, as I knew he carried an M.O. Slowing down, he said, 'Yes, starboard side to,' and stopped his ship. We transferred five men, all of whom afterwards died. It was a tricky situation, as we might have been attacked at any minute.

'Don't be longer than you can help,' said Thompson, leaning over his bridge. 'What sort of a day did you have?'

I couldn't think of a suitable answer except 'Not too bad,' which sounded rather flat and unimaginative.

We were given a respite by the enemy for some hours, and Geoff and I discussed the day and wrote up the log.

When at action stations, as I have already mentioned, No.1

(Geoff) was supposed to be in some safe place in order to be available to carry on if anything happened to me. However, he was always on the top bridge. I pointed this out to him but it never made any difference.

I wrote in the log:

> Tuesday 26th May. Noon position (estimated) 72°30′N. 9°E. Convoy under constant attack. *Empire Lawrence* sunk 1420 hours. Have survivors aboard. Course 060°—speed 10 knots—visibility good—weather fine. Three or four M/Vs sunk, H.M.S. *Garland* damaged.

At midnight the Heinkel III torpedo-bombers returned to harass us, for once a convoy is sighted by the enemy there is no respite. All day long a voice over the convoy's air-raid-warning system would be saying, 'Nine Junkers in section B attacking; twenty Junkers in the sun; enemy aircraft approaching starboard quarter.' The escorts signalled U-boat sightings and attacks and the shad droned mercilessly round the convoy. In the small hours the torpedo-bombers took over the attack.

However, so far, I believe only one ship had been sunk by torpedoes from aircraft, the reasons being that either the attacks were not pressed home or the torpedoes were faulty.

A successful torpedo-bomber attack has got to be the sort of thing the Japs handed out to the *Renown* and *Prince of Wales* in the Far East, or to the U.S.A. at Pearl Harbour. The Germans at this time were trying to operate at too long a range. Latterly they started coming in to about 400 yards and did a lot of damage to P.Q.18, but lost of lot of planes in doing so.

The following day, Wednesday 27th May, the first eleven did not turn out, and the attacks were less effective, otherwise I doubt if any of us would have got through to Murmansk. However, they kept up the pressure and we were closed up at action stations all day as the battle developed.

Being lightly armed, we came in for some special attention from the dive-bombers. I call it 'a near miss' when the ship gets a good shower of spray and heels over. We got a soaking a couple of times, and I think Captain Onslow thought we had been hit, because he came dashing across in *Ashanti* and signalled, 'Are you all right?' We said, 'Yes, thank you.' He made back, 'Come inside me,' which was very friendly, so I took *Lady M* under *Ashanti*'s guns and we had a breather. The sky had now clouded over at about 3,000 ft. which meant you didn't see the dive-bombers until they were on you, but plummeting through the mist spoilt their aim, so little damage was done.

During this day four of the wounded survivors from *Empire Lawrence* died. Sloan, my Irish leading seaman, sewed them up in canvas, weighted with a fire bar. Each man was covered with either an Ensign or Union Jack, and I read the burial service over them before they were gently slipped over the ship's side.

I was unable to bury these four men consecutively, as the service was interrupted by air attacks, and on one occasion, when I had to stop the ceremony and dash back to the bridge, to my amazement I still held the prayer book in my hand open at the burial service.

At noon that day I wrote in the log:

Wednesday 27th May. Noon position 73°35′N. 16°30′E. Convoy still under heavy attack. M/V *Empire Purcell* damaged but no further loss. Course 060°—speed 10 knots. Heavy cloud layer 3,000 ft. Temperature dropping.

Towards evening, at 2000, I heard astern of us that ominous thump that means disaster, and looking aft saw a column of water and orange sparks leap up against the side of the rear ship in the port column. After a ship had been torpedoed it was invariably shrouded in clouds of steam and took on a list, and this is what happened on this occasion. I rang A/S action stations and hurried *Lady M* to the stricken ship.

I love ships of all kinds, and it hurts me to see them destroyed. They lie there in their death agony like some wounded animal. Some take longer than others to die—some sink gracefully and proudly and others break up in a frenzy of despair.

This particular ship was the S.S. *Syros*, and when we got to her she was well down by the bows and her crew had abandoned ship. H.M.S. *Hazard* had arrived before us and was busy picking up survivors. We sent both sea-boats away and collected some more. She was an American ship, and I shall never forget one American seaman standing up alone on a small raft making the hitch-hiking sign to us. The Americans were in very fine form and seemed to regard the whole thing as a joke. I must say that out of some 300 survivors we picked up at various times, a large percentage were Americans, all of whom laughed and joked as soon as they came aboard. One Negro went straight from the life-boat to the ward-room, polished up all the glasses, borrowed a steward's white jacket and appeared on the bridge to ask if I cared for a 'high-ball'.

It didn't take us long to get the *Syros*'s survivors aboard, and in about half an hour we set off to catch up with the convoy. Bill Sedgewick, who was officer of the watch, ordered full ahead, and just as I was wondering how long it would take us to regain our station, Bill suddenly yelled 'hard a-port' down the voice-pipe to the quartermaster, at the same time pointing his hand to port. I saw two torpedoes running in our direction. Bill's quick reaction saved us, and we had the relief of seeing the tin fish go fizzing past *Lady M*'s side. I rang the A/S alarm. Geoff came tearing up on to the A/S bridge. I took over from Bill, whose A/S station was aft, and turned *Lady M* towards the direction from which the torpedoes had been fired. Our senior A/S rating—one Higgins—was a first-class hand and quite imperturbable, and it was music to my ears when he quietly said, 'Contact bearing green 20, strong hydrophone effect.' Geoff, listening on the second hydrophone, confirmed this and started his instruments going. He gave the setting for a ten-charge depth-charge pattern and the crew aft reported back, 'Ready'. McTavish was, as usual, dancing about the 4 in. gun platform, and I went full ahead towards the U-boat, guided by Geoff and Higgins. I also warned the engine-room to 'give her all you've got' and *Lady M*, thoroughly insulted by such a dastardly attack, tore towards her enemy. Perhaps we were getting more experienced, or perhaps *Lady M* took the law into her own hands; the fact remains that we made three book attacks holding the contact right through. Conditions were good and we let go thirty depth-charges in these attacks. The destroyer *Volunteer* came back to help in the hunt.

After our third attack we lost contact and I turned *Lady M* to go back and look for traces of wreckage, oil and the most hoped-for prize of all—a body. We felt very confident, and after some time, when the destroyer signalled us: 'Am in large patch of oil, consider you have sunk U-boat, suggest we both rejoin convoy,' we were satisfied.

Volunteer signalled: 'Make your best speed' and set off at 30 knots towards the convoy. We could steam only 13 knots against the convoy's 10 and as the convoy was now some twenty miles ahead, I knew it was going to take me about eight hours to catch up. When H.M.S. *Volunteer* pulled out of sight the only thing I could see was the distant smoke from the convoy.

Lady M was alone and if we were attacked and sunk nobody would ever know how we met our fate. The weather was now getting foggy, which meant we must be approaching the ice edge; it was getting unpleasantly cold, too. I went to the chart-room at midnight and estimated our position. We must now be approaching Bear Island, and the problem was that in the convoy sailing instructions it had been left to the Commodore and to the escort C.O. to decide whether the convoy should go inside Bear Island or leave it to port, depending on where the spring ice edge turned out to be. As we steamed northwards the weather was becoming more and more foggy. As far north as 73 degrees there is no night, but when the sun was obscured visibility at midnight would have corresponded with 1700 of a September afternoon in London. At 0100 on the morning of Thursday, 28th May, I lost sight of the smoke of P.Q.16 while steaming on a rejoining course of 40 degrees. A little later on we crossed the 100-fathom line, which meant we were some fifty miles away from Bear Island, but just where I didn't know, presumably to the south-east.

I stayed on the same course, hoping that the weather would clear and I would re-sight the convoy as the sun rose higher and dispersed the fog. It also occurred to me that the convoy, taking advantage of the fog, might suddenly have altered course north-ward, with the intention of shaking off the enemy by leaving Bear Island to starboard.

From my point of view the situation was obscure. However, the solution soon settled itself, for instead of the visibility increasing, it lessened and, worse still, we began to encounter a chain of floating icebergs. The cold became intense and our guns and equip-ment started freezing up. I turned *Lady M* towards the east, for had we gone northwards we would have steamed right into the ice barrier. I had lost P.Q.16 and now our only hope of finding it again was to lay off a track which would, next day, intercept the convoy's course. I do not know to this day *Lady M*'s movements on the 28th May 1942. I was forced to steer a zig-zag course to avoid crashing into the huge dark-green shadows which loomed in our path out of the mist. Once, on turning to port, we ran into the pack ice and I stopped the ship, fearing our propeller would get smashed. We fearfully went astern, feeling our way eastwards, until we found the open sea. It was still littered with drifting green icebergs.

Through the fog and the mist we occasionally caught sight of a low-flying German plane and we could hear the continuous gun-fire. This meant P.Q.16 was not far away from us, but I had no means of telling exactly where it lay or what course it was on. Apparently, we were not the only ones who had lost the convoy for, to my surprise, one of the two shads mysteriously appeared and flew directly over us. The pilot and observers must have thought we were with the convoy, for within half an hour several enemy bombers zoomed over us at about 100 ft. We let go with our Vickers and eight Lewis guns and our bullets ripped into one of them, making it take a sudden lurch and emit clouds of thick black smoke.

I continued to edge *Lady M* eastwards and finally got clear of the ice at 0800 on Thursday, 28th May. To my intense relief, at 1000 I sighted the convoy to the SE and rejoined at noon in approximately a position of 74°30′N and 22°E. I would have given a lot to know at that moment how they had fared in the ice off Bear Island and which side of it they had passed.

At noon on Thursday, 28th May, I made only a brief entry in the log:

Rejoined convoy—estimated noon position 73°50′N. 26°E. Course 120°. Weather clearing. Temperature below zero.

Now the convoy had to turn east away from the ice barrier and its attendant icebergs. There was only one course it could steer if it was ever going to fetch up at the Kola Inlet. This was obvious to the Germans and so now the weather had cleared, having re-sighted P.Q.16 they poised themselves for an all-out attack. Even as the crow flies, the convoy still had 500 miles to go and had already been savagely mauled, so the next twenty-four hours were going to be the crucial ones in its fight for existence. The enemy now had the advantage of a shorter bombing run against the tired and depleted convoy, whose escorts were short of ammunition and their crews nearing the point of exhaustion. The shads were back in circulation, the Schlachters were sharpening their knives and the air attacks mounted in ferocity. Ineffective as an A.A. ship, we hectically dodged a rain of bombs. The R/T tried to keep pace with the attacks and once made what I thought was a classic statement. 'Forty torpedo-bombers attacking port quarter. Nine Junkers in section Duff. Fifty dive-bombers in the sun. U-boat surfaced in the middle of the convoy.' On hearing this, I said to the coxswain down the voice-pipe, 'What have we got for dinner?' I learned to my surprise we were to have bully-beef and pickles. 'Any sweet?' 'Sweet F.A.,' replied Turner. And so we steamed along, wondering if the convoy, or any part of it, would ever get to Murmansk.

These attacks were too concentrated and formidable to allow the convoy to escape further disaster, and at 1500 the ammunition ship S.S. *Empire Purcell* was hit, and blew up with a roar of thunder and a blinding flash of orange. The convoy was in dire distress— the butchers were at our throats. Onslow sent out help messages to the Russians for air cover and destroyer support, but nothing happened. An hour later *Ocean Voice*, the Commodore's ship, was struck in the bows and appeared to be sinking. The U-boats were also active on the surface, relying on the air attacks to engage the escorts in A.A. defence. A shower of sparks and a sickening thud sealed the fate of a large freighter near to us, called the *Lowther Castle*. She shuddered and sank with a terrifying gulch, like water going down a drain. We went to where she had been and found nothing—repeat nothing.

The next victim was the *Empire Baffen*. Heavily bombed astern, she reared up like a frightened horse and then plunged, stern first, to the graveyard of British and American ships, which now lies beneath the Barents Sea.

It was clear to all of us that if help of some description did not arrive very soon the convoy would be annihilated. We were like a prize-fighter smashed to his knees, listening to the referee count up to nine. We strained our ears to catch the sound of approaching Russian fighters, but heard only the ominous sound of a shad.

Then it happened.

Far away to the south-east we were able to make out three large destroyers approaching the convoy at full-speed. Were they Russian or German?

In a minute or two we would know the answer. They identified themselves by opening up their A.A. guns on the nearest German planes. We all breathed again, lit cigarettes and grinned at one another. God had sent us help in our extremity but, paradoxically, it had come from a godless people.

I see that I wrote in *Lady M*'s log on Friday, 29th May:

Position 72°20′N and 31°10E, altered course to 181°. At 1120 joined by three Russian destroyers. Position desperate.

This was the turning point of the fate of P.Q.16. These Russian ships had far better A.A. guns than our escort destroyers, and ample ammunition. We were very short of ammo and it transpired afterwards that H.M.S. *Alynbank*, our A.A. ship, had blasted off over 2,000 rounds of 4 in. shells.

I noticed, with pleasure, that the Germans fought shy of the Ruski A.A. gunners and kept well away from them. The Russians used a high-velocity A.A. gun which went off with a high-pitched wang, and, judging from the track of the tracer bullets, had a flat trajectory of at least 5,000 yds. The rate of fire was also higher than our guns.

Heading almost due south, we now had about 400 miles to go. *Lady M*'s log read 1,950 miles.

At midnight the sun was still 5 degrees above the horizon, glowering at me like a sinister Polyphemus. To paraphrase Noël Coward's lyrics—'Mad dogs and Englishmen go out in the midnight sun.' Well, there the wretched orb was, a beacon to incoming German torpedo-bombers and certainly devoid of any romance. I wondered how I was going to explain this to Sally. I was beginning to hate the sight of the bloody thing: it was my enemy—Death in the Afternoon and Death in the Midnight Sun. I thought of it as an orange in a butcher's shop, surrounded by deep-blue tiles. We looked like being the meat on the slab if we weren't very lucky. To hell with the sun!

On Friday, 29th May, as the convoy steamed southwards, tired and exhausted, we were approaching our journey's end, but we felt happier, as Russian air aid had been promised for the next day and our own minesweepers were due to meet us at 0800 in position 70°30′N, 34°E. We knew they would not let us down, anyway.

The Germans, however, had not forgotten that our most vulnerable position for a final attack would be as the convoy approached the Kola Inlet. The question was, would the Russian fighters turn up in time? We had one more day to go as we approached Kildin Island.

Early on Saturday, 30th May, we sighted a skein of high-flying single-engined planes, which we took to be the expected Russian fighters, but they turned out to be about forty Ju.87s from Petsamo, and a vicious dive-bombing attack developed. In the middle of this holocaust, as our gunners joined the A.A. barrage, I noticed a Heinkel 112 seaplane approaching us at sea-level. It just goes to show how wrong one can be, for I thought he was on fire, as there was a red glow under his wings. Seconds later, when his machine-gun bullets began to hit *Lady M*'s smoke-stack, I came to in a hurry. At A.A. action stations in *Lady M*, I was alone on the upper bridge, except for my signalman. We had to grin and bear being shot together. I had a pair of skeleton Lewis guns, which I used as shot guns (not by Holland and Holland, but lightened to be fired from the shoulder, with pans loaded one tracer to three). I seized my No.1 gun and opened up. The Heinkel's tracers were now coming close enough for me to have lit a cigarette from them. There was nothing I could do but to keep on firing and reach for No.2 gun. I yelled to Bunts to lie down. It was like being in a cowboy film. I must say I was more than relieved when the plane swerved off at about 100 yds. range, and crashed into the sea with a splash like a leaping salmon. I then had some bomb-dodging to do from the Ju.87s, but nothing came uncomfortably near us.

That night we had another visitation from the torpedo-bombers, which once again seemed nervous and did no particular damage. One day I must find out if they had torpedo failures.

The next and final day, Saturday, 30th May, is difficult to

describe, as the strain was beginning to tell and either we were suffering from hallucinations or else something very queer was going on, for at times the convoy appeared to be upside down, miraged in the sky (for my own sanity I learned afterwards that this was an accepted Arctic phenomenon).

After steaming 2,200 miles we met our minesweepers at the rendezvous and were overjoyed to see them. It wouldn't be long now before it was all over. Famous last words! I didn't write up the ship's log this day, but I know that soon after the rendezvous, as the convoy approached Kildin Island, M.S.I., the senior officer of the minesweeper flotilla, for some strange reason, took over command of P.Q.16 from Onslow and attempted to split up the merchant ships into a Murmansk section and an Archangel section. The result was complete confusion, and the Ju.87s pounced on the convoy.

We were ordered to join the Archangel section, then the order was reversed. Whilst steaming between the two sections, a low-flying German plane came at us on our beam; I turned towards him and yelled to McTavish, but that wily Scot didn't need any advice from me. He waited until the Hun was about 400 yds. away (during which time I must say his bullets were whizzing past my head) and then let go. That was the end of that. 'Well done, Mac,' I yelled. 'The cheeky so and so,' he replied.

The Ruski destroyers really saved this situation, as, having plenty of ammo, they put up a terrific barrage over the convoy. Now, to add to the confusion, the tardy Russian fighters turned up. I saw several planes crash into the sea, but as the Russians didn't take any notice of their own barrage, or anybody else's, I couldn't tell if they were German or Russian.

Before we had rejoined our section we were dive-bombed and, by the grace of God, I turned the ship the right way. The bombs exploded in the exact place where we should have been if I hadn't altered course. Poor *Lady M* got lifted out of the water and her engine stopped with a shudder. I thought we were hit, and, telling

Geoff to take over on the bridge, I ran aft and down into the engine-room. Here I found Whitehead and the second engineer armed with a spanner about as big as themselves. The chief did not speak, but gave me a look which I understood. All was not well in the engine-room, even the stokers' soot-covered faces looked pale. The engine's main piston had stuck and the chief was about to try and turn it over, in the same way as you crank a car with a starting handle.

The engine-room was full of steam and I had a nasty feeling Lady M had taken on a pronounced list to port. As I stood there watching, there was a thunderous explosion outside and Lady M again took a mighty heave. The chief and the second dropped the giant spanner, and we all panted for breath. The steam escape was worse and clouded the daylight out of the engine-room. Through a wet fog I saw the chief again wrestle with the huge spanner and, with the others, try to heave the engine over its dead centre. As these men, their half-naked bodies covered with sweat, strained away, I knew that if they didn't succeed Lady M was a dead duck. The second explosion I had felt while in the engine-room could only have meant more bombs aimed at Lady M. Now I couldn't move the ship, she was at the dive-bombers' mercy. We were very obvious in our gay camouflage and, don't forget, we had just shot down a German plane. After what seemed an eternity the piston once again began its downward movement.

'She'll go now,' Whitehead said thickly.

'Well done, boys,' I answered and tore back to the bridge.

At 2000 we picked up a Russian pilot at Bolneolski Island, who took us through a boom operated by two Russian women to the Russian submarine base at Polyarnoe. We finally anchored just before midnight on Saturday, 30th May. Never have I been so tired or exhausted, and this was true of all of us in Lady M.

We came back to life at about noon next day. Graham Butcher, the C.O. of St. Elstan, and his officers, came over to Lady M and we discussed adventures. We also went over our reports of proceedings which, as the senior of the two trawler C.O.s, we agreed I should prepare. Here is a note I wrote to Graham afterwards, with his reply:

Lady M

Dear Butcher,

Here is a draft of my report. Any suggestions?

Please let me have it back before we sail—am also sending you some morphia by hand of Officer for which I should have a receipt.

Yrs.

Graeme Ogden.

H.M.S. *St. Elstan*

Dear Og,

Very many thanks for sight of your report. I think it exactly right and trust it receives the attention which in my opinion it deserves.

B.

I think we were all very surprised, firstly to be alive, and secondly that the convoy had arrived with comparatively so little damage. We could hardly believe that both our little ships had made this dangerous passage unharmed and without loss of life. We were wondering what to do with our survivors, when Lieutenant-Commander Jim Elliot, who was the first lieutenant of the base at Polyarnoe, boarded *Lady M*. He was the last person I expected to see, and I don't know whether it was Jim or I who was the most surprised. It's a long way from Trinity Great Court to the Kola Inlet.

After hearing about our adventures and having a drink to celebrate our safe arrival, he told me to land my survivors at Murmansk, and later that day we steamed up the Kola Inlet to discharge them. I was curious to see Murmansk, which I had heard so much about. When we got there I found that the town was perpetually on fire, as the Germans came over every day and bombed it. The Ruski A.A. gunners, try as they might, could not keep the enemy bombers away, as it was only twenty-five miles to the German-occupied territories.

With the exception of a few large concrete buildings (including the Arctic Hotel), Murmansk was made of wood—and wood burns. The wharves were also of wooden construction, and were, as we were to find out, usually alight. The Russians didn't seem to mind for there is plenty more wood locally, and as soon as they could put out the fires, they built new wharves. On this particular day our illusions of getting any peace or quiet were rudely shattered, as no sooner had we tied up at Murmansk than the German planes came over and all sorts of things began to happen. The Ruski A.A. barrage was a mighty affair, and they did not believe in just firing at odd bombers. They waited until the enemy planes got inside their defence box, and then let go, with a hundred guns. This shook the whole earth for miles around, and my first experience of these salvoes staggered me. We all know the old tag 'whatever goes up has to come down', but at Murmansk you didn't know what had gone up or what was to come down. We saw planes come plummeting down, some into the wooded hills which they had set on fire, others splashing into the river. One plane crashed not far from us, and set the adjacent wharf on fire. Bits and pieces of other planes came hurtling down, including an engine which smashed through the quay a few yards away from us.

As soon as we had landed our survivors, we steamed over to visit Hickman, the C.O. of *Hyderabad*, to see what adventures they had had. Amongst other things, they told us a good shad story. Apparently, somebody in one of the destroyers called up a shad on his Aldis lamp and signalled in English, 'For God's sake go the other way, you're making me giddy,' whereupon the shad replied, 'Anything to oblige,' turned round and circled the other way. They had also made contact with a shad and said, 'Thanks for the air cover,' and got the reply, 'Am leaving you now.' After drinks and a yarn, we steamed back to Polyarnoe, which was very peaceful after Murmansk.

Next day at noon we received a visit from Captain Onslow and Commander Thompson. They came aboard, and Onslow had a short talk with the ship's company, in which he said he was as proud of *Lady M* as any ship under his command. We then retired to our ward-room and discussed the trip over a glass of gin. Onslow told us he calculated he had had 228 sorties flown against us. He also told us that on 27th May, when we still had another three days of battle ahead of us, nearly a quarter of the convoy had been lost and the remaining precious freighters with their deck cargoes of tanks and aircraft, which he had so far successful guarded, were in jeopardy. The promised Russian air cover had not materialized, and if the Germans had pressed home their torpedo-bomber attacks P.Q.16 would have suffered incalculable damage, if not annihilation. As it was, the convoy had lost seven ships, four more had been severely damaged—including the Commodore's ship, the *Ocean Voice*, which had a hole in her bows you could have driven a bus through.

H.M.S. *Garland* had lost twenty of her crew and was lucky to be afloat. Captain Onslow also told us that he and his escort destroyers were perilously short of ammunition. Supplies would have to be sent from England.

I asked him what course the convoy had steered on approaching Bear Island, and explained what had happened to *Lady M*. He said that on running into the ice much to the south-east of where they had expected to find it, the convoy had formed into two columns and had much the same experience as we had, eventually leaving Bear Island to port.

Considering what could have happened, I think Onslow was very relieved P.Q.16 and its escorts had not suffered more severely. I was sorry to learn from Commander Thompson that the wounded

I had transferred to H.M.S. *Martin* had all died. But nobody can live long in those icy seas, even if only slightly wounded.

Captain Onslow asked for my report of proceedings and recommendation for awards, which afterward resulted in Whitehead getting the D.S.M. and Bill and Geoff being mentioned in dispatches. You can't give everybody medals, but I would have liked to give mine to *Lady M.*

The following afternoon I waited upon Rear-Admiral Bevan, who was the S.B.N.O. (Senior British Naval Officer) North Russia, and was most kindly received. He was a harassed man, having much to cope with and his office being on duty twenty-four hours a day, so I didn't stay long. Our convoy had arrived, but he still had on his hands a large percentage of the crews of the *Edinburgh* and other north Russian casualties.

Nobody had any ammunition; food, coal and oil were problematical. The wounded had to be accommodated in makeshift hospitals, ships had to be unloaded and turned round. The Arctic air was thick with W.T signals from Admiralty, wanting to know the details of convoy P.Q.16.

The Russians were being very 'Russian', and had refused to admit a hospital ship which had lately arrived. The Admiral gave me our signals and here they are:

C.O. LADY MADELEINE   ACIC
Herewith your signals. I am very pleased to have seen them and to have your report. You certainly went through it and you and your ship's company did remarkably well. I will forward a copy of your report to C.-in-C. H.F.

To: Escorts and Ships of Convoy P.Q.16
From: Commander-in-Chief, Home Fleet.
My heartiest congratulations and great admiration for the gallant way they fought their passage through in the face of strong and persistent opposition. I sympathize with them most sincerely in their loss of their fine shipmates.

Distribution

      Commodore A.N. Gale. R.D.

      N.C.S.O. for Allied Merchant vessels (25)

      Allied escorts.

Authenticated

      J.B. WARD. Pay. Lieut-Commander, R.N.V.R.

      Secretary to Senior British Naval Officer, North Russia.

C.-in-C. H.F. (R) Escort ships of P.Q.16 *Ashanti.*

Thank you very much for your 1101B/31 which is greatly appreciated. We are proud to have brought the convoy through and estimated 228 sorties with enemy aircraft.

The courage and determination of the Merchant ships was beyond praise. 1232B/1

General Kola Inlet

From: Senior British Naval Officer, North Russia.

The First Lord of the Admiralty and The First Sea Lord congratulate all officers and men of the Allied Merchant Navies and Allied Forces concerned on their magnificent exploit in fighting Convoy P.Q.16 through to North Russia in the face of all the enemy could do in the air and at sea.

      T.O.O. 1801B/31

Distribution

      Commodore A.N. Gale, R.D.

      N.C.S.O. for Allied Merchant vessels (25)

      Allied ships and submarines of the Escort Force.

Authenticated

      J.B. WARD, Pay. Lieut-Commander, R.N.V.R.

      Admiral's Secretary.

It was now June and the sun was up for twenty-four hours a day. The wooded hills either side of the Kola Inlet were covered with a blanket of snow, and day temperatures were just above freezing point.

Polyarnoe, the Russian submarine base, was a small deep fiord off the Kola Inlet. The latter runs south up to Murmansk, the head of the railway which eventually arrives at Leningrad. The place itself has a long wharf behind which rise some huge concrete buildings and within these half-derelict structures were housed the British Naval H.Q. and also the Russian naval authorities.

Polyarnoe, being surrounded by high hills, was easier to defend from air attacks than Murmansk, which is in flat open country. It could hardly be called an attractive place at the best of times, but it did contain a broken-down concert hall and an Anglo-Russian naval officers' club. It was here I met Captain Gale, our Commodore; his ship *Ocean Voice* had survived the hit which had blown a huge hole in her bows, but he told me the foremast had crashed on to the upper bridge and pinned him on his back.

I remember his saying that, although he had always opposed welded ships in the past, no riveted ship could have survived the damage done to *Ocean Voice*.

The first job we did for Admiral Bevan was a scrounging party to try to get some food off the merchant ships for the stranded seamen ashore. The American ships were very well supplied and most generous, so we came back some days later with our foredeck piled high with food—not that we hadn't traded a little gin to get it, U.S. ships being officially 'dry'.

Next we had a whip round to try and raise towels, toothbrushes, cigarettes, matches, combs, bandages and medical stores for the R.N. hospital. Then we had to coal from the merchant ships, using baskets, and this took us about five days to complete in a continual air-raid.

The moment had now arrived when we were to meet Skipper Lieutenant Drake, R.N.R. Commanding Officer H.M.T. *Chiltern*. In other words, 'Skipps'.

Skipper Drake, as broad as he was tall—and he was not very tall—was eternally cheerful and used language which would have caused a stir on the fish wharf at Hull. The *Chiltern* was a small trawler, which fetched up in Russia for some strange reason, and had become a maid of all work. In air-raids, snow-storms, fogs, blizzards, night and day, Skipps drove the *Chiltern* up and down the Kola Inlet. One of his main troubles in life was that his superiors did not give him enough time for his tea.

'I had just tied up alongside when the old man wanted me to go up to Vaenga. Well, I was having me tea. See what I mean?'

One day Skipps waved a bottle of beer at a Russian soldier. The man said, '*Da, da, pozhalooista,*' meaning, 'Yes, please,' so he gave him the beer. Ever after this, Skipps was in the habit of inviting me to have a *pozhalooista*. It was he who told me that there were some Husky puppies ashore, and that if I went to a certain address I might be able to get one. This is how Roubles came into my life. He must have been about five weeks old when I carried him under my duffel-coat back to *Lady M* and was the furriest little ball I've ever seen. By the time he was a year old he looked like a mixture of a chow and an alsation, but when I first had him he looked like a teddy-bear. His mother was so tough that she never came indoors at all, and had her litter in the snow, and the Russian who sold him to me said his pa had been a wolf. Strange to say, Roubles was the gentlest of dogs, with a sweet temperament, until we went to action stations, and then he rushed up to the bridge and barked like a fury.

One day we had a football match against some Russians. This was remarkable, for the ground on which it was played was a valley from which the snow had been partially cleared. It was littered with huge stones and contained two open wells and its only resemblance to a soccer ground was in the goalposts. The Russians, for some strange reason, sent a military band, which played merrily away and gave the game quite a festive air, reminding me of halftime at the Cup Final. It was certainly the queerest game of soccer in which I have ever played. The ball would drop down a well, bound on a rock at odd angles or at times even get buried in the snow. Almost everybody playing got hurt, and I regret to say we lost the game.

"Tis not in mortals to command success. But we'll do more, Sempronius—we'll deserve it.'

Another effort at sports was more successful. Five ships' companies took part, and we had the usual races with the addition of a 'Charlie Chaplin'. This was new to me. You have to carry an empty tin canister between your legs, twirl a cane and balance a sailor's cap upside down on your head over a distance of 50 yds. If you drop anything you have to stop and start again. The race was full of comic possibilities, which were appreciated by the audience and commented on in naval and Russian language.

We were suddenly distracted from these amusing diversions when we were ordered to make a trip to Archangel. The voyage I shall describe later in this story, but the sight of this northern capital of the Tsars was tremendously impressive.

Why or how this city ever came to be built, I don't know. The interesting thing is that, although it was in a bad state of repair in 1942 when I saw it, years ago it must have been a fairy-tale city, sparkling in the snow. There were all the remains of stately palaces and churches with their gaily painted 'onion' domes. There were tree-lined boulevards, trams and villas. Now it was a grim and sorrowful place, but at the beginning of the century it must have had an icy and mysterious grandeur. In 1919 we had invaded the place to oppose the Bolsheviks and suffered a severe reverse. Knowing this, it seemed very queer to be there twenty-three years later as a Russian ally, but to be more accurate not an ally of the White Russians, whom England had backed.

When we returned to Polyarnoe we found we were just in time to take part in a Russian sing-song at the Krasne Theatre. I think *Lady M*'s team stole the show, for the Russians were quite fascinated by Turner's 'I stuttered too much' and by Gaunt singing 'Mr. Wu'—à la George Formby. Most astonishing to me was the musical genius of the Russian sailors' choir. Every man an artist... how does this happen in the desolate frozen north?

What shocked me was the crude and bizarre posters which lined the theatre foyer. These, presumably rather out of date, depicted Americans murdering children and Roosevelt as 'Satan'.

The ammunition for the homeward convoy Q.P.13 had now arrived, and we were given the unenviable job of distributing it to the merchant ships. *Lady M* was loaded up until you couldn't see her decks and it took us three days to go the rounds and visit some twenty ships.

In order to minimize the danger of air attacks, these ships were strung out from Vaenga Bay to Murmansk, a distance of some twenty miles. The trip up to Murmansk and back was a hazardous one for two reasons. First, the Russians (as secretive as ever) only gave one the barest idea of where their local minefields were, and the leading lines they gave were avenues cut in the snow-covered forests. Second, *Lady M* had now become an ammunition ship and, as I had seen S.S. *Empire Purcell* blow up with the loss of all hands, I wasn't keen to have the same thing happen to *Lady M*. It wasn't for the lack of trying that the German bombers from Petsamo did not achieve this. Had they hit us, the homeward-bound convoy could not have sailed.

When we had finished this task 'to S.N.B.O.'s satisfaction' we were ordered to anchor in Vaenga Bay. This suited me very well for the first lieutenant of the fleet minesweeper *Gossamer* was a friend of mine and we had a lot to talk about. It came as a gruesome surprise to learn on arriving that *Gossamer* had been hit by a bomb a few hours earlier and had apparently been lost with all hands. If there were any survivors I never saw them.

H.M.S. *Boadicea* had hastened to the scene and so had *Beagle*. These two destroyers had come north with P.Q.15 and were homeward bound with Q.P.13.

That evening I was invited to dine aboard *Boadicea* and, after the usual gin session, I sat down to dinner next to a tall fair-haired midshipman, who seemed vaguely familiar to me. About halfway through the meal I was pretty certain that this was the young man who had bowled out the Harrow side, and also made the winning hit, in the Eton and Harrow match in 1940 which I had seen while on leave.

I was right, the midshipman turned out to be Antony Gibbs. Marooned in north Russia as we were, I think we both enjoyed talking about Eton and its images. Just to mention the 'Burning Bush', Absence in the school yard, Lupton's Tower, Upper Chapel, the Provost, the block and birches, Tom Bubb in the school stores, fish-cakes at Bunkers, The Field and The Wall, did us good. We didn't feel quite so remote. We talked of playing cricket on long afternoons until the shadows of the trees on Upper Club fell across the pitch. We spoke of Sheep's Bridge, Jordan, Mespots, South Meadow and the 4th of June, when the Guards band lazily played the 'Boating Song' punctuated by the sound of the bat and the ball. How, when the glorious day was over and the last of the fireworks had exploded, tired and happy, one went asleep dreaming of some friend's sister. But 'my tutors' and 'your tutors' didn't mean anything to the rest of the assembly, so we had to return to naval matters.

The story of the evening concerned the C.O. of *Boadicea* who, after dining aboard *Beagle*, inadvertently walked into the icy sea. His boat's crew fished him out and took him back to his ship. A few minutes later he appeared in the wardroom crackling like a brown-paper parcel, his clothing having frozen up, and downed a few drinks. He then took a hot bath and was none the worse for his adventure—an iron man if ever there was one.

About midnight the party broke up and I stepped very carefully into my boat before I was rowed back to *Lady M*.

Lady M returned to Polyarnoe and carried out various tasks for Admiral Bevan, including de-fooding a derelict merchant ship. While we were at it, we helped ourselves to an oerlikon gun, which later on Mac mounted on *Lady M*'s engine-room casing. We took 'a spare' as well.

On 25th June the convoy conference for Q.P.13 was called, the convoy's date of departure being fixed for 27th June. Two Russian submarines were joining the escort for some of the way and, as we were lying near them, I was ordered to make sure they understood the convoy sailing instructions. I therefore invited the two captains aboard *Lady M*, who duly arrived with an English-speaking Russian sailor who looked exactly like Jack Sharkey. We went to my cabin and I enquired what they would like to drink. They chose whisky, so I sent for Squires to fetch up a bottle. This lasted about five minutes and Squires' face was a sight to behold when I ordered a second bottle. Geoff appeared and the five of us accounted for three bottles before the Russians left. I must say I enjoyed the get-together, but I can well see it must have been a terrible morning for Squires.

Q.P.13—and '13' is an unlucky number for me—sailed at noon on 27th June 1942. The convoy numbered thirty-five merchant ships, with our old friend Captain Gale as Commodore. The close or 'through' escort was much the same as that of P.Q.16 plus some fleet minesweepers going home to refit and the two Russian submarines.

In *Lady M* we had six extra crew who were survivors from the *Edinburgh*. They were looking forward to seeing home once again; we were, too, if it came to that, but unfortunately we were bound for Iceland, my *bête blanche*.

The weather was overcast and, for once, the sun which had been the undoing of P.Q.16, only naturally in reverse, so I will not give our route, positions, etc. It is enough to say that the weather began to thicken and the wind rose. We steamed south-west through thick patches of fog which swirled around the convoy, cutting visibility down to half a cable. It was a weird and ghostly experience hiding in this murk, and praying the enemy wouldn't spot us. On Tuesday the 30th the weather cleared and to our dismay we had a visitation from a shad.

This aircraft did not stay long with us, and I think he was really looking for the next northern-bound convoy, P.Q.17, which had sailed from Hvalfiord the same day as we had left Russia. I hoped we would see it off Jan Mayen Island where the north- and south-bound Russian convoys usually crossed, as Leo and Dick in *Ayrshire* were part of the escort.

The wind dropped and the weather became foggy as Q.P.13 stole along unmolested in the eerie Arctic silence. We passed Jan Mayen Island on 2nd July and apparently crossed P.Q.17's track without seeing them. This latest northbound convoy, consisting of thirty-five merchant ships, had a very strong escort with it in view of the knocking about we had taken in P.Q.16. It had a covering force of battleships, Admiral Hamilton's cruiser screen and a close escort of some dozen minor warships, which included Captain Lawford in the A.A. ship *Pozarica* and Captain Broome in H.M.S. *Keppel*, plus three rescue ships, which were old friends of ours from Atlantic days.

All I noted in the log the first day was that the weather was so foggy we had not seen P.Q.17, but that two fleet oilers had joined Q.P.13. On our way southward Geoff and I kept wondering how P.Q.17 would fare when they came into the 'attack zone'. The presence of our battleships looked as if the Admiralty was expecting the heavy German ships based in Norway to make a raid. With Haliday's aid, we kept a W/T watch on P.Q.17's activities, thus on 4th July received a signal from the Admiralty addressed to P.Q.17, ordering the convoy to scatter (T.O.O. 2215/4/7). This, we thought, could only mean the worst had happened and the *Tirpitz, Scheer, Lützow* and *Hipper* must have been at sea and approaching the convoy. Having plotted P.Q.17's probable course, its position at this time was ironically enough some 100 miles south-east of Hope Island in about 75°55′N and 28°40′E, that is to say, around 500 miles due north of the tip of Norway.

Soon we picked up distress signals from the beleaguered merchant ships of P.Q.17, now fighting lone battles for their existence a thousand miles to the north of us. We in *Lady M* thought a major fleet action was about to be fought and listened in anxiously for news of it. I thought of Dick Elsden and Leo in *Ayrshire* and was reminded of having been scared half out of my own wits by being at sea at the time of the *Bismarck* incident. Nobody at this time realized that the report of a German battle squadron being at sea in northern waters was incorrect and the scatter signal was therefore unnecessary.

On 5th July, still in foggy weather, Q.P.13 divided into two sections. Commodore Gale, in *Ocean Voice*, which had been patched up in a Russian shipyard, left with fifteen merchant ships, together with the destroyer escort, and headed south-south-east towards Seydisfjörd and so onwards to the U.K. The remaining nineteen ships with a reduced escort, consisting of Commander Cubison in *Niger*, Senior Officer, plus *Hussar, Hazard, Roselys, St. Elstan* and *Lady M*, proceeded westwards. Captain Hill, in the American *Robin*, was the Commodore of this western section of Q.P.13. The weather had been so thick that no navigational sight had been possible for days and nights on end, resulting in the convoy's position being only an estimated one, and hence unreliable after such a long passage. However, the fleet minesweepers and the corvette with us had good radar sets (the 271 Magnetron, 10 cm. wave type) which promised to be adequate to make a landfall on the Icelandic coast. So we set off for Reykjavik in good heart.

When the Q.P.13 split, our section was given a course of 266 degrees to steer, but no estimated position was given. I made our own position 67°40′N and 15°W. The wind began to rise and soon a north-easterly gale had blown up, bringing with it a heavy ground swell. We were enveloped in low vaporous clouds and visibility was down to under a mile. *Lady M*'s position was on the convoy's port beam.

At 1830 the convoy was re-formed from a broad front into two columns, *Hazard* and *Hussar* leading the way with *Roselys* and *Niger* astern. The course was altered to 222 degrees.

At 2000 I came up on to the bridge to keep the first watch with Geoff, and was just in time to see *Niger* sheer off to port flying a signal hoist we couldn't distinguish.

At 2040 I saw *Niger* come steaming out of the gloom and take up a position about half a mile off our port bow. She made a V/S signal to pass on to the Commodore to steer 270 degrees. While the signalman was busy calling up the nearest ship, there was a heavy muffled explosion and, on looking round, I saw *Niger* had taken on a heavy list and was clearly in serious trouble. I made a hurried entry in the log:

H.M.S. *Niger* torpedoed 2040.
Estimated position 66°30′N 23°10′W.

I then took *Lady M* at full speed to *Niger*, broadcasting as I went that *Niger* was sinking. It was now a wild noisy evening but as *Lady M* plunged towards *Niger* I heard to starboard a quick series of heavy explosions. Through my glasses I could see merchant ships stopped and apparently sinking.

By the time we got to *Niger*, her bows were pointing skyward like a toy boat. The part of her bottom which was above water was unharmed. I thought at the time an acoustic torpedo must have blown her stern off. Some of her crew were clinging to the nearly perpendicular foredeck and others covered in black oil were hanging on to a Carley float some little way away. Within a minute, with a final hiss of escaping steam, she slid backwards into the hungry sea and disappeared before our astonished eyes.

The heavy sea running made it necessary to get to windward, thus making a lee and drifting on to the raft. (A ship beam to wind will drift much faster than a waterlogged raft.) *Lady M*'s stern just missed the raft, but a heaving line was grabbed by the men hanging on to it and now began the struggle to get these men aboard. In those days we did not carry scrambling nets to help survivors climb inboard, and the task of rescuing those oil-covered sailors from the raft as it rose and fell in the heavy seas was heart-breaking.

I left Geoff on the bridge and went aft to help get *Niger*'s men aboard and actually had my arm round her oil-covered Australian first lieutenant when a wave swept him away never to be seen again. Apart from saving his life, if we had got this man aboard we might have solved the mystery of *Niger*'s fate. As it was, the men we did get were engine-room ratings and very bemused as to what had hit their ship. As far as I know, all of her officers perished including Commanded Cubison, her captain.

During this time the gunners on the merchant ships had opened fire indiscriminately, under the impression their ships had been attacked by U-boats on the surface or a German raider. Shells were whining in all directions and raising water-spouts as they pitched into the sea.

I went back on to the bridge to join Geoff and manœuvre *Lady M* alongside another raft which we had seen. Just as we started to move, someone aft yelled, 'Torpedoes running starboard quarter,' so Geoff went full ahead and hard a-starboard. Looking aft, I saw what I took to be the track and bubble wake of two torpedoes. I had seen plenty of torpedoes one way and another, and I remember noting that these two were rolling and burrowing their way through the waves, which meant they had been fired at long range and were slowing down.

The convoy was now in a state of utter confusion. Nobody knew what was happening. Merchant ships were firing at one another, or anything they could see in the water, which was dotted with life-boats from the sinking ships. *Hazard* and *Hussar* had disappeared into the fog with the leading ships and remained silent. We never saw the van of the convoy again. Graham Butcher, in *St. Elstan*, thought we had been attacked by U-boats on the surface using gun-fire and torpedoes. So did I, as apart from having seen torpedoes I had seen a merchant ship which was stopped, hit fore and aft by shells. Conversation was difficult with *Roselys*, the French corvette. I believe Lieutenant Bergeret, her captain, thought we had run into a minefield, but I couldn't see how this could be possible. Firstly, because while on the same course the van of the convoy had steamed over the same ground unharmed, and, secondly, from the state of the sea, we were clearly within a few miles of the land. A quick look at the chart showed me that on my reckoning we were roughly on the reverse track P.Q.16 had taken going north-east. Unless somebody had sown a new minefield while we had been away in Russia, the only one I knew of, and which was shown on our minefield chart, was miles away to the north-east in the Denmark Strait. On the other hand, it would have been too simple for U-boats taking advantage of the fog to collect and lie in wait for the convoy which they knew was bound for Reykjavik. The only other possibility to my mind was the presence of a German cruiser.

I decided to make an anti-submarine search, and steamed round the five sinking ships in a wide circle. The two senior officers were ahead in *Hazard* and *Hussar*, *Roselys* was a Free French corvette and *St. Elstan* was another trawler, so the three of us did what we considered best in these appalling circumstances.

We in *Lady M* picked up some strong Asdic contacts and made several quick attacks, more with the idea of letting any U-boats in the vicinity know we were after them than in hopes of scoring a direct hit. This operation over, we returned to the centre of the wreckage and began to pick up boat-loads of survivors from the American merchant ships. Unfortunately, they were mostly inexperienced seamen and terrified by the huge seas. They rowed for the sake of rowing, not looking where they were going or watching the treacherous waves. Some of them even pulled to my weather side and broke themselves to pieces against the ship.

The first boat-load I got on board contained, amongst others, Captain Dalton of the S.S. *Hybert*, who handled his sea-boat in such a way as to allow me to rescue him. He was very cool and collected, and when I asked him how his ship had been sunk he told me that he had been hit by heavy-calibre shells. From what Dalton said, it sounded as if a German raider had attacked the convoy, so I sent off a signal to A.C.I.C., quoting his report. On the other hand, I still considered that five ships being hit simultaneously was more likely to be the result of a salvo of torpedoes. I never expected to survive that night and the next morning. We spent hours and hours picking up and searching for survivors. Had we been in a minefield, we should have assuredly been blown up. If U-boats were about we were a sitting target, and if a raider was present we were helpless—our only chance was the fog.

We continued with the rescue work, and by early next morning our decks were crowded with survivors. I had steamed about all night without trying to keep any dead reckoning, so had little idea where I was, especially as the convoy had never made a landfall. I had a conference with the American officers and we set a course to the south-east to look for land.

At 0600, while on this course, I saw through the half-light a dim shape to starboard. I said to Geoff, who was beside me, 'What do you think?'

We looked at the shape through our glasses, and saw it was a heavy cruiser travelling at speed.

'It's a German raider,' I said suddenly, feeling rather sick. We both stood there, waiting for the first salvoes. There was none of those crisp words of command one comes across in films and books; we were both far too frightened to say anything. After what seemed eternity the cruiser flashed us with her powerful signal-lamp and my heart went bumpity bump as our signalman took the message. The 'raider' was one of our cruisers, the *Kent*, which had been sent to our assistance in answer to my signal to A.C.I.C. Geoff handed me a cigarette, which I lit with a shaking hand. Her C.O., Captain Cunningham Graham, was most disappointed I could not give him any accurate information about the presence of a German raider.

After giving us a position, he went off at speed, searching to the northwards.

I don't know to this day exactly what happened on that ghastly night, and I don't think anybody else does either. One explanation is that we ran into a minefield, but if that theory is correct a lot of things don't add up. I would give a lot to know the truth.

In a few minutes the losses of Q.P.13 became comparable to those of P.Q.16, which had battled its way far into the Arctic against the fury of the enemy. As will be seen from my joint report with Graham Butcher, Q.P.13 lost five large merchant ships and H.M.S. *Niger* on the evening of 5th July. Here is my letter of proceedings to Admiral Dalrymple-Hamilton, who was then A.C.I.C.:

To: A.C.I.C.
From: C.O. *Lady Madeleine*
Date: 9.7.42
Attack on P.Q.13 (Western Section) off North Cape of Iceland.
Submitted: Estimated position 66°28′N. 23°35′W. Sea 46. Wind N.W. force 7. Visibility M 4 ships station, port beam of convoy.

1.   At 1815 hours on 5 July convoy altered course from 266° to 222° and formed into 2 columns. At 2220 hours H.M.S. *Niger* signalled Commodore Hill in *American Robin* to alter to 270°. *Niger* left on course of approximately 170°. At 2040 hours *Niger* returned and took station on my port bow. Distance 4 cables. At 2043 hours *Niger* blew up and took a heavy list to starboard.

2.   Within 3 minutes 4 M/Vs were stopped and sinking. I saw a 5th ship hit by torpedoes.

3.   I took *Lady Madeleine* to *Niger*'s assistance and rescued some of her crew.

4.   At 2258 I made a signal to A.C.I.C. saying I considered Q.P 13 had been attacked by U-boats. I then carried out an A/S search.

5.   I later picked up survivors including Captain Dalton and the officers of the S.S. *Hybert*.

6.   These officers were convinced they had been sunk by heavy shells from a German cruiser. I therefore made a further signal to A.C.I.C. suggesting presence of enemy surface raider. T.O.O. 2340.

7.   We searched the area for survivors, U-boats or a possible enemy cruiser until 0400 when owing to the weather I lost touch with the situation, and decided to make a landfall to find out where we were.

8.   At 0600 hours next morning I saw land and also H.M.S. *Kent* which I mistook for an enemy ship. They made V/S contact with us, but I had no definite information for Captain Cunningham Graham.

9.   Having established our position we proceeded to Reykjavik independently and landed 32 survivors.

10.   Although I understand it is considered that this convoy ran into our own minefield to the N.W. of the Cape of Iceland I do not accept this supposition for the following reasons:

(a)   The leading 14 ships passed unharmed.

(b)   H.M.S. *Niger* was well to port of the convoy.

(c)   From E.P. which I confirmed by making a landfall we were nowhere near the known minefield.

(d)   I am convinced I saw one M/V torpedoed.

(e)   *Lady Madeleine*, *St. Elstan* and *Roselys* steamed about in the area for many hours without exploding any 'mines'.

11.   According to my information the following ships were lost:

> H.M.S. *Niger*
> S.S. *Hybert*, U.S.A.
> S.S. *Michigan*, U.S.A.
> S.S. *Mona Key*, U.S.A.
> S.S. *Rovina*, U.S.A.
> S.S. *John Randolph*, U.S.A.

12.   It is regretted we were not able to rescue more of the *Niger*'s crew.

> Signed. W.F. OGDEN
> LT. R.N.V.R.

It looked as if in the last six weeks about fifty ships and probably some 1,500 men had been lost on the north Russian convoys. The 'Kola Run' was now known as the 'Murder Run' and it seemed obvious that no more convoys would sail until air support could be provided. Another thing was that it would be much better to sail the Russian convoys from the Shetland Isles where there was an air base from which cover could be provided for at least half of a much shorter voyage.

We stayed in Reykjavik for another two weeks, in which we pulled ourselves together and straightened out the ship. We were then ordered home.

BOOK THREE

CLOUDS AND DARKNESS

The voyage home took us to the Faroe Islands and then down the east coast of Scotland to the River Humber, for soon after leaving Iceland we had been re-routed to Grimsby and told we were to refit there. We made the passage alone and in fine weather. To sail over a thousand miles in midsummer through the northern latitudes is an unforgettable experience. The sun made it arc in a pale blue sky over an even paler sea until it finally disappeared behind a curved rainbow-coloured horizon. At night the ship's wake sparkled, leaving a luminous trail behind us.

At times, to the accompaniment of the swish of the waves, I could hear the melody of Debussy's 'Au clair de lune' endlessly repeating itself through my head.

When the moon rose up out of the 'steep Atlantik stream' its reflection in the sea contained for me moments of supreme enchantment, as there I fancied my tired eyes could see an image of Sally's exquisite beauty.

As we steamed homewards from these distant waters, a surge of excitement began to grip the whole ship's company. A major refit meant leave for everybody, and leave at Grimsby was most welcome, as many of the crew came from those parts. Thoughts of the yellow cornfields of Lincoln, the smell of fresh grass, of an inn standing beneath high elms, went through my head, for these were the things I had missed so much.

Lady M needed no encouragement from me to make a quick passage—she had been born at Hull and that was the chief's home town too. 'My Sea Lady', as I was beginning to call her, tucked up her skirts and ran homewards as fast as she could go.

On the evening of the fifth day after leaving Iceland, we rounded Spurn Head and caught the evening tide up the muddy river to Grimsby. It seemed that almost everybody in *Lady M* knew the way to Doeg's shipyard and so we tied up there in record time and went ashore to drink in the pubs and feel the English earth under our feet.

We were delighted to receive a telegram from our friends at

the Bank of England who had adopted us as one of their protégés congratulating us on our success:

The dockyard and admiralty conference was held in the afternoon, to which Geoff and I went with light hearts, as we had been through all this before at Ardrossan. All we wanted were two new Oerlikon guns and a new phosphor-bronze propeller for *Lady M*, as her cast-iron one had got chipped in the ice, plus, of course, a long list of small additions. Alas, we received some news which brought us up with a round turn. It transpired that the object of this refit was to convert *Lady M* for 'winter conditions in the Arctic'. Nothing could have been more unwelcome. This meant, among other things, that all steam-pipes would have to be heavily lagged, the stern of the ship strengthened against ice, water-tanks protected from freezing up, steam heaters provided for the guns and a general disembowelment of the ship.

Geoff and I looked at each other in disgust; we both had had quite enough of north Russian convoys and the idea of spending the coming winter on that run appalled us. We could only envy Mac and Bill, who were leaving *Lady M* for service elsewhere.

For the next few days Geoff and I had plenty to do. We said goodbye to Mac and Bill, sent the crew on leave and in the evenings tried to catch up on how the war was going elsewhere. On 4th June the Americans had fought it out with the Japs in the Battle of Midway. In June the Japs had launched an all-out attack on Burma, and now in August Rommel and his Afrika Korps were nearly into Egypt. Our shipping losses were as bad as ever and the

Russians were pegged down by the Germans 1,500 miles inside their own boundaries. The situation didn't look too good. The R.A.F. had, however, started raiding Berlin and Hamburg, which was some consolation.

I had written to Sally the day after we had arrived in Grimsby, but had not had an answer. This didn't surprise me, but as soon as I could get away I went to London to look for her, and also to make plans to visit my mother who lived in the country near Oxford. I reached London on Saturday afternoon, and hastened to the theatre to try to find Sally. Long before I got there I knew something was wrong, either she wouldn't be there or else...? Shaftesbury Avenue looked much the same, but when I turned a corner my heart ceased to beat and my whole body froze. Where the theatre should have stood was a huge pile of rubble, surrounded by wooden trestles. Above, black iron girders criss-crossed the sky. When I could speak I questioned a newsvendor. 'When did it happen?' I asked, pointing to the wreckage. ' 'Bout three weeks ago, terrible disaster...lots of people killed...'

'Miss...Miss...Sally...C-Carlton?' I stuttered.

'Don't know, guv. You mean the little red'head, don't yer? Nice girl she was...often used to buy her papers off me...No, I can't 'elp yer, I'm afraid...better ask at the station.'

'Thanks, Charlie,' I said, and bought a newspaper.

I didn't go the local A.R.P. station; I hadn't the courage just then. I took a taxi to Duke Street, where I climbed the well-known steps to the flat and found half a dozen full bottles of milk. I banged on the door like a lunatic, knowing Sally wasn't there and hadn't been there for days, or perhaps weeks. If she were dead, to all intents and purposes I was dead too. I had to find out what had happened, so there was nothing for it but to drag myself to the nearest A.R.P. station. This turned out to be a section of the Green Park Underground. After asking several distracted wardens, I was shown into the room where I should make my dismal enquiry. This looked like Captain Stanhope's dug-out in *Journey's End*. The walls were piled high with sandbags and behind a trestle table sat a grim-looking officer wearing a steel helmet with a gasmask slung over his shoulder. On the table was a litter of papers and an empty whisky bottle with a candle in it. Above the desk was an electric-light bulb in a wire cage and somewhere in the room a red light was glowing. The officer, on closer inspection, appeared to be an elderly major in the Home Guard. He wrote steel glasses and his face was drawn and tired. He looked up from his papers.

'Yes, is there anything I can do for you?'

'I came to enquire about the damage done about three weeks ago to the Duke of Devonshire Theatre in Shaftesbury Avenue.'

'You mean about the casualties? A very bad show that. Sixteen people were killed, and thirty injured. The bomb went right through the roof during an evening performance.'

I thought I was going to be sick.

'Was Miss Carlton damaged—I mean injured?' I managed to ask. 'Any identification?'

'My God,' I suddenly thought, 'identification.' Supposing Sally had been killed still wearing my identification bracelet?

'She had red hair and blue eyes.'

He looked at me irritably. 'I haven't got the lists here,' he said. 'Come back tomorrow. I'll make a note—Miss Carlton.'

I turned to go, but he beckoned me back.

'Why aren't you wearing a steel helmet and carrying a gasmask?' he barked at me. 'There's an alert on, you know.'

'I'm sorry, I didn't know.'

'How do you think we can make civilians obey orders if people like you in uniform disregard them?'

His cold eyes looked me over from head to foot. I had smart-ened myself up and put on my new uniform for Sally's benefit and, with no medals on my chest, it occurred to me I probably looked rather green, but when his eyes came to rest on Sally's delicate identification bracelet on my left wrist I saw him wince.

'It's time you learned something about the war,' he said gruffly, 'and set a good example to others, or perhaps you're one of these tough sea-dogs,' he added sarcastically.

'I won't forget again, if you'll only—'

'You had better go into the shelter until the raid is over.'

'Thanks, yes, I will,' I said, and stole out into the gloom.

I began to walk towards Berkeley Square, with no particular object, but my feet carried me to the flower shop from where I had so often sent her flowers, but that was in the days when the nightingales sang and one wore a white tie and tails. As I began to cross the deserted gardens, the guns on the A.A. site in Green Park opened up.

For want of anything better to do, I sat down in the fading light under one of the ancient plane trees which stand in Berkeley Square and then remembered gloomily that the square had originally been a plague pit. My depression was not lessened when shrapnel splinters began to crash into the foliage above me. I decided the A.R.P. warden wasn't such a prig after all, but strangely enough, as the crescendo of London's A.A. barrage increased in its intensity, I began to feel more at ease. I lit my pipe and decided to sit out this noisy dance with *Lady M.* as my partner. Later, when things had quietened down, I got up and headed for the Naval and Military Club. I was both hungry and thirsty, but here too I found the enemy had struck. Two bombs had wrecked the entrance hall and bar, killing some of the members. 'Gandhi', the imperturbable barman, refused to be 'put out' and thought nothing of it. The members were having their drinks. Shakily I asked Cook, the porter, if there was any mail for me. He handed me a letter from Sally. I couldn't see the date of the postmark, but on tearing it open I saw that it was dated 17th August—that was a week ago. I went into the garden and read the letter. It told me of the holocaust of the burning theatre, of her miraculous escape and her decision to join E.N.S.A. and to go on a tour of North Africa. I don't know how long I sat in the garden, but it was pitch dark when I went into the remains of the bar where I joined the crowd. Partly out of relief that Sally was alive, and partly to drown my misery and disappointment at not seeing her and being with her, I started drinking. Hours later I staggered into Stratford Street.

Here I encountered a friendly black-and-white cat. 'Hullo, cat,' I said, 'are you alone too? What about some dinner?' Cat gave a mew, or was it a purr? I said sternly, 'Why aren't you wearing your steel helmet and where is your gasmask?' Cat rubbed itself against my legs. 'Another thing, too, if you're a sea-faring cat you're a very bad example to civilian cats, or,' I added sarcastically, 'perhaps you're one of these tough mouser cats.

'It's about time you learned something about the war,' I said, as I picked it up and walked to Curzon Street. Here I turned into a restaurant and to my utter surprise saw Ernest, who used to be the head waiter at the Berkeley Hotel. We greeted each other as long-lost friends.

I explained I wanted a table for two—for myself and the cat, which I had christened Whiskers. It should be put on record that Ernest never blinked an eyelid. 'But of course, Mr Ogden,' he said, and gave us a table. I ordered some fish for Whiskers and something for myself. The cat was obviously a well-bred cat, for it sat on its chair and behaved quite beautifully. In our loneliness we comforted each other and I fell in love with her. She was later to have kittens in my cabin, just before we sailed again for Russia, and she and her family made the trip with me.

N ext day I caught a train to the country and went to my mother's home. The house stands on a bend of the river and 300 years ago was an inn for bargees. There is a lagoon where the lawn ends through which the lazy stream flows. Surrounded by tall poplars and yew hedges, clipped into monstrous peacocks, in summer it is a dream house. Sitting on the lawn drinking tea with my mother, and wandering in the rose garden at sunset, made me conscious of what I was fighting for.

A few months ago I had been in the Arctic Circle, where there are no trees, no green fields, birds or flowers. Although in summer the sun shone, it was rather as if a searchlight had been turned on to illuminate a ghostly, volcanic landscape. I tried to tell my mother what north Russia had been like, but sitting beside the peaceful Thames and listening to the coo of the doves made any description of mine sound unreal. I told her that apart from the Russian armed forces, the inhabitants of Murmansk and Archangel seemed like people from another planet. You couldn't tell the men from the women. Some had Mongolian faces, others were fair-haired and blue-eyed. I looked at my mother's fragile beauty. Could some of these people I had seen in northern Russia really have been women? It seemed impossible. On the other hand, the Russians were so tough and determined that, although the Germans were at that moment victorious, provided enough of them were well armed, I felt sure they would drive the Germans out.

I remembered Admiral Burrough telling me a story about his visit to Moscow after P.Q.16 to see 'Uncle Joe'. They apparently had a tremendous dinner together in the Kremlin and drank so much that the Russian chiefs of staff and generals eventually slid under the table. Stalin then turned to Admiral Burrough, who was still under control, and said to him: 'You see what a lot of rotten generals I have. They can't even drink.' My mother was 'not amused' by this story.

I stayed for some time in the dreamy Thames Valley and on Sunday we went to the village church where I had been christened. There nothing had changed. Time and wars meant nothing to this ancient place of worship, which had been in existence during the days of the Spanish Armada. Listening rather drowsily to the vicar's sermon, my mind went back to the services I had held abroad *Lady Madeleine*. I could see the crew mustered aft, the ship lifting to the Atlantic swell, and the wide arc of the sky above us. I could hear the lusty voices of the crew singing the hymns and remember myself reading Lord Nelson's prayers. Divine Service at sea seemed more real to me just then.

The sermon didn't hold my attention and I admit my mind wandered off to north Russia and the voyage we had made to Archangel earlier in the summer. We had sailed round the snow-covered coast of the Arctic in terrifying silence. To seaward we had seen the pack ice and in the distance the blue ice-wall itself. The sea had been as still as a millpond and the ship's wake had stretched behind us like a scratch on a sheet of glass. Archangel had turned out to be a ghost city, which I have already described. I remembered I had bought some furs for Sally and gone on a tram ride... I was shaken out of my reverie by the churchwarden nudging me with the collection bag.

When *Lady M* sailed out of Grimsby in late September I was very pleased with her, and although I had failed to get any more guns, our 'gash' Oerlikon now was correctly mounted aft. I had changed coxswains and Addsets, a deep-water man, had replaced Turner. We were bound for Tobermory, once more to work up before returning to Belfast and then going to north Russia for the winter. Once a ship has been to Tobermory it ceases to be quite so alarming, and as I knew my crew, I thoroughly enjoyed our stay there. Lieutenant Ken Forth and Sub-Lieutenant Thompson had replaced Mac and Bill, but Geoff remained with me as No.1. In spite of the fact that we were all experienced hands, when the fatal day came for passing out we got ourselves into a first-class muddle and once more the Commodore had the best of us. However, this time he refrained from jumping on his cap, and made a very encouraging speech to the ship's company and wished us good luck.

I took *Lady M* to Belfast in October, where we had not been since February 1941. Steaming up that blue-green loch with its stimulating memories was to be a homecoming.

> 'Oh! Dream of joy! Is this indeed
> The lighthouse top I see?
> Is this the hill? is this the kirk?
> Is this mine own countree?'

When I went to wait upon the Flag Officer, I found to my delight it was Admiral Bevan, whom I had last seen in Polyarnoe.

We stayed in Belfast doing local convoys for the next two months, and I was gratified to find that Leo Gradwell and Dick Elsden were also there in our old friend H.M.S. *Ayrshire*. It was there I learnt some more of the story of the ill-fated convoy P.Q.17 which we, homeward bound in Q.P.13, had passed off Jan Mayen Island as it sailed northwards to disaster. Earlier in this story I have related my own misgivings about this convoy, but I can now tell you the part which *Ayrshire* played in this ill-omened voyage, as related to me by Leo and Dick.

The strategy was that the enemy, encouraged by their success against P.Q.16, had decided that they could and would annihilate the next Murmansk convoy. They had learnt, however, that a determined escort could get a proportion of a convoy through, in spite of all they could do by the use of dive-bombers, torpedo-bombers and

U-boats. Doubtless they had calculated that to wipe out a convoy it would be necessary to separate the escort from the convoy by drawing it off with surface craft, then the merchant ships would be entirely at the mercy of their U-boats and aircraft. This, to a very great extent, is what did actually happen but, as a result of a false estimate by the Admiralty in Whitehall of the movements of the heavy German ships based in Norway, and not as a result of their sailing to attack P.Q.17. Here is Dick Elsden's eye-witness account which he has been kind enough to write down for me:

'For the first few days we had much the same sort of time as you did. An early sighting and then regular circling by shads. But we were lucky in having a fair amount of fog, and early on the 4th July, when all the American merchant ships hoisted flags in honour of Independence Day, the convoy passed north of Bear Island with only one ship lost.

'As with you in P.Q.16, we had a covering force of cruisers, but it remained to the north of the convoy and was sighted only occasionally. One of the cruisers used to send her Walrus aircraft over to see how things were going. On its last visit it was chased round the convoy by a shad, and eventually had to come down. The trawler *Middleton* picked up the crew, and then took the Walrus in tow. When *Middleton* reached Archangel, she still had the Walrus astern. It must have been an awfully dead Walrus by that time.

'During the 4th July the fog cleared and, in the evening, there were heavy air attacks in which two ships were sunk and the Russian tanker *Azerbaidjan* set on fire. Aboard *Ayrshire* we reckoned she had had it, although her guns continued to blaze defiantly at the departing aircraft. Some of the German aircraft preferred to pick on the trawlers, stationed well out, rather than face the concentrated fire of the convoy which, Graeme, is no surprise to you. Leo was hard put to it to dodge torpedoes fired at him from three directions simultaneously. In spite of his twisting and turning, one ran so close along *Ayrshire*'s port side that I could have read the maker's name without glasses.

'As the second attack ended, a report was received from the Admiralty that the *Tirpitz* and other heavy units had sailed from a Norwegian fjord and were approaching the convoy. The inference was obvious. The report was followed by direct orders from the Admiralty, with priority "Most Immediate", that the convoy was to scatter. Moreover, the covering cruisers, already due to leave the convoy, were ordered to retire at speed to the westward, and the destroyers of the close escort were ordered to join them.

'Two submarines which had been with the convoy so far were ordered to take up patrol positions to the south, and the remainder—merchant ships, two A.A. ships, corvettes, mine-sweepers and trawlers—were all to make their own way as best they could, alone and independently, to Archangel, still 800 miles away. It was certainly a grim outlook, for that "Most Immediate" convinced everybody it could only be an hour or so at the most before *Tirpitz* and her consorts came over the horizon. Even so, there was a moment of light relief when one of the submarines signalled the senior destroyer, *Keppel*, that she intended to remain on the surface as long as possible. *Keppel*'s reply expressed the general feeling: "So do I."

'In fact the *Tirpitz* had not sailed to attack the convoy, although she did so a little later. By then, however, the enemy found her task had largely been done for her, and she was recalled. In the meantime the ships were fanning out, some to the north, some north-east, some east, and some to the south of east, for the essence of the order to scatter was that there should be as much distance as possible between each individual ship. Leo, however, as he watched them disperse, was convinced they were all heading for disaster. He decided therefore to ignore the order, and take two or three merchant ships with him.

'The chart showed, away to the north-west, a small island called Hope Island, and Leo's plan was to lie up close to it until the worst of the enemy's fury had died down, and then cut and run for Archangel. Accordingly, he collected the two nearest merchantmen, *Silver Sword* and *Troubadour*, and set course for Hope Island. A little later he collected a third ship, *Ironclad*. Two were American, and the third Panamanian.

'The next thing was to prepare to meet the *Tirpitz*, but first Leo "spliced the main brace", and issued a warming tot of rum all round. Then, with everybody munching corned beef sandwiches—we did not expect to have much time for eating later—all the depth charges were primed and set, and oil drums secured to some of them with long wire strops. The idea was to place *Ayrshire* across *Tirpitz'* bows and hope that, when she sank, the ensuing explosions would cause some damage. Finally, every 4 in. shell in the magazine was stacked on the gun platform, so that the maximum number could be fired with no delays over ammunition supply.

'We never reached Hope Island. Instead, about midnight, although with the sun of course still well up, we came to the Polar pack ice. Leo turned his small convoy east, along the edge of the ice, but very soon the W/T reports from ships being attacked showed there was no future in that direction. Leo therefore turned north again and, using *Ayrshire* as an ice-breaker, he cut a channel some twenty miles or more into the icefield, through which the merchant ships could follow. Eventually the ice became so thick that *Ayrshire* could break it no more, and we were all forced to stop.

'I then went aboard the merchant ships, walking across the ice to each in turn. I found they had tanks on their upper decks, and investigation showed the ammunition for their guns was all ready in the racks inside. Accordingly the gun barrels of suitably placed tanks were cleared of their protective grease, and crews were arranged to man them in case of attack. Firing such unusual broadsides might not do much good, but at least the noise would be encouraging.

'I also found all three ships had plenty of white paint so, on my return to *Ayrshire*, orders were given for all the ships to paint the side facing south, and the upper decks and funnels. Every available man was put on to painting, and using deck-brooms as brushes the camouflaging was completed within an hour. Then, with fires banked to leave no tell-tale wisp of smoke, we sat down to wait. Hour after hour we listened to the W/T reports, S.O.S. Bombed, S.O.S. Torpedoed; we could feel explosions reverberating through the ice, and even see a column of smoke rising in the still, clear air, as some unfortunate ship blew up. We saw too that strange Arctic phenomenon of an inverted sky mirage. Enemy aircraft were flying along the edge of the ice, but they never noticed those four odd-looking hummocks in the icy waste.

'Two days later Leo and I decided it was time to move, but this proved difficult because a southerly breeze has packed the ice tight against the ships. Eventually, however, we reached clear water where, to our relief, we saw a bank of fog only a few miles to the south. Scarcely had we reached it when an aircraft flew low directly overhead. Aboard *Ayrshire* everyone held his breath, hoping none of the merchant ships would open fire.

'We felt it was still too risky to head direct for Archangel, so Leo stood on to the eastward until we reached an open bay near the north of Novaya Zemlya, where all four ships anchored. *Ayrshire* was now very short of coal, and several tons were transferred from one of the merchant ships, their white paint in the meantime making the ships inconspicuous against a glacier background.

'When coaling was finished, Leo decided to coast down to the Matochkin Shar (or Matthew Strait) which runs through the middle of Novaya Zemlya, and then go through to the Kara Sea. The only snag seemed to be that, according to the Atlas—we had run out of charts and were using a *Times Handy Atlas*—there was a Coast-Guard Station at the entrance to the Strait and it was thought quite probably this would be in enemy hands. The simple solution would obviously be to capture the Station and accordingly, before we sailed, plans were made for a landing party which would include some of the gunners from the merchant ships.

'Unfortunately, as we rounded up in to the Strait, one of the merchantmen ran on rocks. Worse still, as *Ayrshire* went to her assistance, she also struck the rocks. We got both ships off, but *Ayrshire*'s Asdics were put out of action. While this was going on, my landing party had pulled ashore, scaled the cliffs and assailed the Coast-Guard Station. Instead of the fusillade of shots we expected, we were received with coffee and buns.

'*Ayrshire* dared not use her own wireless but, with signs and words of one syllable, we managed to persuade the Russians to make a W/T signal to Archangel, in code, advising of our arrival, and requesting A/S escort, because we were told there was much U-boat activity off the coast. From the Russians we learnt the Kara Sea was completely frozen over, but as it was obviously too dangerous to remain near the entrance to the Strait, Leo led his ships as far up the Strait as they could get. He then anchored the merchant ships close under high cliffs where bombing would be difficult, a wise precaution because we were soon sighted by enemy aircraft.

'Of our adventures during the following days, while waiting for the A/S escorts, I can deal only briefly, for it is a story in itself: our encounter with a Russian ice-breaker aboard which we were shown a film of the Russian Revolution; another salvage job, this time with the assistance of the Russian Trawler *Kirov*, during which *Ayrshire* sustained further damage; a run down the coast and then wading waist deep in the ice-cold water to pick up survivors who had reached the coast. We also collected another merchant ship— the *Azerbaidjan*. When *Ayrshire* last saw her, shortly before the scatter, she had been torpedoed and was blazing furiously. Now, apart from the gaping holes in her sides, and buckled decks, she looked as if she had just left dock, and the same applied to her crew, both men and women.

'Eventually the corvettes which had been with P.Q.17 arrived in the Strait, bringing with them the Commodore of the Convoy, Commodore Dowding. His ship, the *River Afton*, had been sunk following the scatter, and he was wearing army battle dress and a Junior Naval Officer's cap, but there was nothing junior about the man who, for all he had been through, had nevertheless set forth to bring in the remainder of his flock.

'After a short conference to plan courses and speeds and dispositions, we set sail. Shortly after we left, U-boats arrived in the Strait, no doubt to finish off the remnants of the convoy which the aircraft had spotted but, thanks to Leo's careful anchoring, had been unable to bomb. Finding them gone, they vented their wrath on the Coast-Guard Station, although with what effect Leo and I never heard; in Russia, at any rate in those days, you didn't hear. As for the ships, perhaps it was a tribute to their endeavours that they all reached Archangel without incident, except *Ayrshire*. As we came to the bar of the Dvina River she ran out of steam; she had burnt her last nugget of coal—we had even swept out the bunkers with brooms—and the merchant ships could spare her no more. But she, and her ships, were there, and we gladly accepted a tow from a corvette up the river.'

No doubt the dire fate of P.Q.17 will be discussed long and often after the war is over. All one can say now is that there must have been considerable confusion somewhere on a high level. As far as I know, out of the thirty-six merchant ships which sailed from Iceland, only eleven reached Archangel, and—worst luck—still five of these were sunk by bombs while at anchor; this leaving only six survivors. Leo Gradwell got a D.S.C. for his part in this action and Dick Elsden and his crew must go down in history as a gallant company of resourceful and brave men.

> '"I fear thee, ancient Mariner!"
> Be calm, thou Wedding-guest!
> 'Twas not those souls that fled in pain,
> Which to their corses came again,
> But a troop of spirits blest.'

Well, for me that is the best way to think about P.Q.17.

I t was now November and time for us to get ready for the winter convoy, which was to be called J.W.51 and to sail from Loch Ewe on the north-west coast of Scotland about the middle of December.

We collected our Arctic clothing and cold-weather supplies from the base and also found to our joy that 'The Establishments Branch of the Bank of England' had sent us all manner of good and useful things.

We sailed from Belfast for Loch Ewe on 7th December and anchored there two days later. While making this passage, I wondered about what was likely to happen to *Lady M* in the next few weeks and what I should be prepared for.

One knew pretty well what to expect from the enemy, but I didn't know what to expect from the weather. Small ships have been known to be lost owing to their weather side icing up to such an extent that they could remain upright only with a strong wind on their beam, but if the wind suddenly shifted they capsized.

I knew it was going to be excessively cold, but what was the effect of intense cold going to be on the ship and her company? Would the water-tanks freeze? How long could the look-outs stay on the bridge? Would the depth-charges and guns ice up so as to make them unserviceable? The more I thought about this operation, the more I disliked the whole idea of it.

Although after Prien had taken his U-boat in Scapa Flow and sunk the *Royal Oak* Loch Ewe had become a fleet anchorage, it was a makeshift sort of place and in 1942 the naval base consisted of a few Nissen huts. It was in one of these cold and bleak places that on the 14th December 1942 the convoy conference for J.W.51 took place and as usual was presided over by the Naval Control Shipping officer. After P.Q.17, one more summer convoy had been attempted, but with dire results, and so the effort had been given up until now, when it was thought a small convoy might slip through in the prevailing darkness. The convoy J.W.51, we learnt, was to sail in two sections. We, with *Northern Wave*, were in the first half, with Captain Scott-Moncrieff in H.M.S. *Faulkner* as S.O. of the through escort. The second half of the convoy was to sail on 24th December, the day before we were due to arrive in Russia. The close escort for this later section was to be under the command of Captain Rupert Sherbrooke in H.M.S. *Onslow* with five other 'O'-class destroyers. These ships were of new construction but poorly armed and this is worth noting in view of what was to happen to J.W.51B. The merchant vessels in this convoy were limited to sixteen in each section. Nobody seemed to know why we were now labelled 'J.W.' instead of 'P.Q.', but we hoped it would change the luck anyway.

Back in *Lady M*, Geoff and I went through the convoy instructions and made our sailing preparations. Considering the prospects of this trip, I found the crew in good heart, milling around the ship whistling 'I'm Dreaming of a White Christmas'. They were going to see enough ice and snow to satisfy their wishes for a lifetime, but fortunately they did not know it.

We sailed from Loch Ewe with J.W.51A at 1500 on 15th December 1942. The Commodore was Rear-Admiral Turle, who led fifteen ships out of Loch Ewe into the murk and gloom outside the anchorage.

True to form, as we stood by at our sailing stations dressed up in our new Arctic clothing, over the ship's loud-hailing equipment came the sounds of 'She's off in the North'. This, of course, made me think of Sally, and as I stood on *Lady M*'s bridge listening to the reel which kept time with the throb of the ship's propeller, and watching our new White Ensign flutter bravely astern, I felt a glow of satisfaction. We were off on as tough a voyage as any ship had ever undertaken. The phantoms who had visited me that first night I had slept aboard *Lady M* had in their time the unknown to contend with, but we had something else as well—the Germans. I made the necessary entries in *Lady M*'s log and turned in.

Loch Ewe is 58 degrees north and in mid-winter there are only about six hours of daylight there, and as we sailed northwards these hours were going to be reduced every day until there would be only a red smudge on the southern horizon at noon.

The convoy cleared Cape Wrath in the small hours of 16th December and went on to a course of 030 degrees. The weather was crisp and clear, with little wind and practically no sea running. At night we witnessed displays of the Northern Lights or the aurora borealis. In fact, at times it was lighter at night than in daytime.

Our noon position on 16th December was 61°30′N and 3°W. Course was altered to 010 degrees. Looking at my chart, entitled 'The Greenland and Barents Seas' (No. 2282), which I noticed had been first produced by the Hydrographical Department of the Admiralty in 1872, I saw that this course would take us to Jan Mayen Island. This was practically the same course we had steered on our summer convoy but in winter the pack ice would have receded. So from now onwards I will not give our day-to-day positions. What really mattered was the weather and the ever-increasing cold. Many of us have read about earthquakes and have some sort of idea in our minds of what it would be like to be in one, but yet have not had the physical experience of being personally involved. Going north into the Arctic winter was something I had thought about, and studied what conditions one might expect to find, but their actual occurrence still came as a shock to me. By the time we had been at sea for a week and were south of Edward Island, although we had not been attacked by the Germans, we had suffered severely from the Arctic climate. It seemed incredible that seven months before we had sailed over the same course in perpetual daylight and that now we were shrouded in darkness beneath menacing black clouds, with only a few hours of sickly daylight. We were either enveloped in heavy snow-storms, which fell relentlessly for days, blotting out the outlines of the ships in convoy, or being lashed by icy gales which suddenly roared down upon us.

In *Lady M* we soon found that the Admiralty's specification for 'Arctic conditions' was quite inadequate. Apart from chipping the ice off everything above decks, we discovered that the guns froze up, the wireless aerial collapsed, the depth-charge rails were solid with ice, the winches cracked and even the rudder chain had to be continually de-iced with steam jets. Worse than this, if you touched anything made of metal with your bare hands it took all the skin off them. To avoid frostbite the only practical thing to do was to cover one's face with engine grease, or goose grease if you had any. The whole question of existing became a problem. Trawlers were designed for fishing and the crews lived in the warm belly of the ship near the boiler-room, where they could keep warm, eat in comfort, dry their wet clothing and have a good night's rest. The Admiralty experts who converted these ocean-going trawlers to anti-submarine vessels put the officers' wardroom, cabins and mess for'ard in the fish-hold. The only entrance or exit to the officers' quarters were via a companionway which led on to the foredeck. This meant that all food had to be carried along the main deck from the galley, which was aft of the engine casing. Never a practical arrangement, in Arctic conditions this method of messing broke down completely. Similarly, my cabin was the coldest place in the ship, being on the main deck below the bridge. The sides were made of steel and if I managed to get up any kind of a fug the warm air condensed and froze on to the bulkheads. The only two who seemed impervious to the cold were my Russian Husky puppy Roubles and Whiskers, the cat from Curzon Street. It didn't seem to matter how much extra clothing one put on, it still did not keep you warm. I found Roubles and Whiskers, who had become great friends, the best sort of hot-water bottle at nights. Certainly more effective than Squires' effort, which by the time it had arrived in my cabin was frozen solid.

As we drove our ships through the snow and ice, *Lady M* took on a fantastic appearance. 3 in. wire stays became the size of 12 in. fenders. Icicles draped the upper bridge and you could have skated on the decks. The only consolation was that no U-boat or aircraft could operate in these conditions. However, in the darkness an enemy surface raider might appear at any minute. So far we had been unmolested.

As one may read in the *Arctic Pilot* (which I may say had been my constant companion on the way up): 'In mid-winter the mouth of the Kola Inlet is often fogbound, especially with a south-westerly or south-easterly wind. A north wind brings gales, an east wind cold and clear weather and a south wind brings snow.' It was snowing when we arrived early on Christmas Day. As we steamed up the inlet, I passed Hal Clouston in *Cape Mariato* and also Bob Pate in *Argona*, so we yelled at each other and arranged to meet later in the day. We anchored just before the Mitchicoff light, and, sure enough, later on *Cape Mariato* and *Argona* came alongside, and so began Christmas Day of 1942. Hal told me that he had gone on the last summer convoy (P.Q.18) and that they had had an aircraft-carrier with them whose planes had fought off the attacking German aircraft, but I gathered the convoy had had a pretty sticky passage all the same, losing several ships. In order words, whatever you do in daylight, if the convoy is going to be within range of enemy aircraft for ten days and nights, near U-boats and heavy-surface-craft bases, a convoy has to run the gauntlet and fight its way through. All the same, it was disappointing to learn that P.Q.18 had had such a bad time, as I happened to know that in August, in an effort to soften up the German air base on the Norwegian coast, H.M.S. *Glorious* had lost a large percentage of the planes she flew off—about sixty, I think.

But back to Christmas Day in the Kola Inlet. That day it was even colder than it had been at sea, but, full of rum and whisky, we thoroughly enjoyed ourselves. Next day Hal and Bob sailed homewards. They had done their share, now it was our turn. I scribbled a note to Sally and gave it to Hal to post in England, but I had to address it to E.N.S.A., London. Perhaps she would get it months later after a concert to the troops in North Africa. I could visualise the scene only too well. The brown jobs in search of amusement—and what else?

I had received an invitation to dine with Admiral Fisher, who had replaced Admiral Bevan, and so had Mathews of *Northern*

Wave. Going down the inlet in the dark was a very different business from our summer trips, and I had great difficulty in finding my way. The Kola Inlet runs between high ground on either side and has landmarks which are easy enough to recognize in summer, but when covered with snow in winter they assume a uniform appearance, which makes navigation a dangerous business. It was unbelievably cold, and, standing on the bridge, when I tried to blow my nose I broke some icicles off instead. I had also grown a beard on the way up and now found this had frozen up.

I got *Lady M* down to Polyarnoe about 2000 in a blizzard. (In winter it's nice and warm in North Africa, I believe.) I couldn't even recognize the place. There was a strong off-shore wind (about force 7) and the result was that it took me two hours to get *Lady M* tied up alongside. With about two minutes to spare, in my best uniform I went ashore through a blanket of snow to S.B.N.O.'s house. There I had a good dinner and met Captain Scott-Moncrieff, who had been our S.O. coming up. It was the first time I had been warm for weeks and I enjoyed the friendly atmosphere. I tried not to think about North Africa.

We talked about north Russian convoys in general and wondered how Captain Rupert Sherbrooke, the S.O. for J.W.51B, who had sailed from Loch Ewe on Christmas Eve, was getting on. What none of us could understand was the Russian attitude to our efforts. We had all noticed that crates of war material we had brought up in the summer were still on the quays and now half-hidden in snow. Murmansk itself seemed to be inhabited by a regiment of lost souls who shuffled through the gloom like 'living sacks'. I learnt most of these people were condemned to slave labour and consequently took as little interest as possible in the proceedings. If they showed open revolt, or got too weak even to pretend to work, the Russian guards shot them and didn't even bother to bury them. The Russians also made life difficult and unpleasant for our own ships' companies, both ashore and afloat. The survivors from the *Edinburgh* I gathered had had a ghastly time of it and many had died quite unnecessarily for want of medical supplies and living conditions. All these things made it very difficult to understand the Russian mentality and war effort. God knows, I had read Dostoievsky, Pushkin and Maxim Gorky, but hadn't the picture changed since then? It may have been that we were on a far northern outpost, but one couldn't help feeling that the year was probably nearer to 1842 than 1942. I think we all felt the same about it, but 'ours is not to reason why...' so we enjoyed our dinner and drank up good and hearty.

On the morning of New Year's Day, 1943, I went to the naval base at Polyarnoe and found the place in a high state of excitement. Signals had been coming in for the last twenty-four hours which indicated that J.W.51B had been attacked by enemy battleships on the morning of 31st December. One heard snatches of conversation to the effect that Captain Sherbrooke had been killed in action, that several destroyers had been lost and words such as 'Scharnhorst', 'Hipper', 'Tirpitz' being indiscriminately hurled about. Everybody wanted to know where our heavy ships were and what had happened to them. Bob Burnett seemed to have been here, there and everywhere. The only good news was that the convoy appeared to be intact. This time there had not been any scatter signal, and the gallant Sherbrooke's destroyers had fought a battle against what appeared to be fantastic odds and succeeded in protecting the convoy. I stayed around for some time trying to get a more accurate account of what actually had happened, but failed to do so.

I returned to *Lady M* with a feeling that 'it had to happen'. Ever since the murder of P.Q.17 the fear of an attack by heavy German ships had been in the minds of those on the Kola run. Well, now it had happened and nobody could feel very surprised about it. All one could hope for was that our losses were not as serious as they sounded.

I was soon to find out, for on the morning of 3rd January I was ordered to take *Lady M* alongside H.M.S. *Onslow* to deliver medical supplies and take off some of her wounded. This was Sherbrooke's ship. In the half-light, when I found her, it was hard to recognize her as a destroyer. She was lying against a wooden wharf with a background of ice and snow, her grey-and-white camouflage concealing some of her damage, but I saw her foremast was down, her bridge shattered and there was a large jagged hole amidships. When I went aboard her quarter deck I could see she was riddled with shell-splinters and I marvelled how she had kept afloat after the battle and managed to steam onwards to her destination.

I gathered from her officers that Captain Sherbrooke had been hit in the face by a shell-splinter, and had lost the sight of one eye and now very possibly both. The plan was to get him back to Scapa Flow in a flying boat—if such a thing existed in north Russia or could be got from home in time to save him. I took the wounded to the hospital in Vaenga Bay.

H ere is the story of J.W.51B as I have pieced it together, but why the second half of the same convoy was attacked and not the first half, which we were in, is something I shall never know.

The German plan seems to have been to send the heavy cruiser *Hipper* with some destroyers to the north of the convoy route, then attack it with the idea of driving the convoy southwards, where the pocket battleship *Lützow*, with more destroyers, would be lying in wait. This plan very nearly succeeded, as our cruisers had got too far away to the north-east, and if it hadn't been for Sherbrooke and the other destroyer captains, aided to some extent by the weather, this plan might have proved lethal to the convoy.

Apparently, in the weak morning light of 31st December, between snow-storms, Lieutenant Hickman, R.N.R., in the corvette *Hyderabad* (a companion of ours on P.Q.16), sighted some German destroyers and soon after this the *Hipper* came on the scene. She fired at H.M.S. *Achates* and scored a hit. *Northern Gem* went to her assistance and took off seventy of her crew before she sank. At this time Skipper Aisthorpe told me he made his position about 73°N and 30°E. Captain Sherbrooke in H.M.S. *Onslow*, with the four other destroyers (*Oribi* being out of touch), attacked the *Hipper* and the German destroyers. Sherbrooke got hit about noon and handed over to Commander Kinlock in H.M.S. *Obedient*. Soon after this the C.O. of the corvette *Rhododendron* got the shock of a lifetime when he saw the *Lützow* to the south of him. (I should say here that the convoy had turned southwards away from the *Hipper*, as anticipated by the Germans.) By the grace of God, H.M.S. *Sheffield*, with H.M.S. *Jamaica*, now arrived from the north-east and engaged the *Lützow*. A violent snow-storm blotted out all visibility at this period and the German ships broke off the action.

Jack Angleback, in the trawler *Vizalma*, had had a night-mraish time, for having got separated from the convoy with a single merchant ship earlier on, he suddenly found himself in the middle of a fierce naval action. One of the saddest parts of this story was that the minesweeper *Bramble*, who found herself on her own in this action, got blown to pieces by German shells and was sunk with all hands in the freezing Barents Sea. It was also very depressing to know that our old friend *Achates*, from the Clyde Escort Force, had gone down with heavy loss of life.

Captain Rupert Sherbrooke was awarded the Victoria Cross for his part in the action and many other officers also won decorations. The rather sketchy account I have given here of the battle for the safety of Convoy J.W.51B was put together in 1943 from information I received from the commanding officers of the small ships who took part. It now appears in naval history that Hitler was so infuriated by the failure of his heavy ships to fight it out with the enemy that he ordered they should not put to sea again, and that their guns be transferred to the West Wall.

What fascinated me at the time was that although *Lady M* had not taken part in this battle, we had passed through exactly the same area only a few days before, and so I was familiar with the conditions in which the battle had been fought. I could feel the tenseness of the drama which had existed for the survival of the merchant ships. I could visualize the ghostly shapes of the enemy ships suddenly emerging out of the gloom, and the unexpected salvoes of shells and gun-flashed. I could see Sherbrooke's destroyers tearing through the brown water in line ahead, preparing for a torpedo attack, and then finding their target obliterated by a sudden snow-squall. This fantastic game of hide-and-seek in the Barents Sea must have been the most nerve-racking sea battle ever fought.

In this eerie holocaust the Commodore, Captain Melhuish, and his merchantmen steamed slowly along in a series of snowstorms like a flock of sheep pursued by a pack of wolves.

Sherbrooke, as gallant a man as there ever was, couldn't possibly have known what he was up against in the early stages of this battle. All he could have known was that with five destroyers his duty was to fight off German surface ships, which might well have been a battle squadron consisting of the *Tirpitz*, the *Scharnhorst*, the *Hipper* and the *Lützow*. His genius lay in menacing the German ships with his torpedoes but not firing them, for, once he had done so, they had nothing to fear. Although Admiral Burnett's two cruisers were steaming at full speed to his aid, Sherbrooke must have been driven almost insane wondering when they would appear on the scene of action.

As I saw the picture, Sherbrooke and then Kinlock were snaking their destroyers at full speed between the *Hipper* to the north and the *Lützow* to the south, dashing from one danger point to another, never knowing when they might encounter the enemy forces. I felt then and I feel now that this scene must never die—even if nobody else ever writes about it. The thought of Sherbrooke directing the battle, severely wounded and in great agony, must remain an inspiration to future generations of naval officers. Sherbrooke, although hopelessly outgunned and wounded, attacked five times but withheld his torpedoes.

I n small ships the problems of food, coal and water are always
with you. The only Russian coal available was not coal to our
way of thinking, but a mixture of peat, ice and rocks. The local
water was infected and had to be boiled before being used for
cooking or drinking. Russian food consisted of bread and a little
meat, which might be horse or yak. Things hadn't changed since
our last visit, so the S.B.N.O. told us to look after ourselves,
which was fair enough, and I sailed next day with the idea of
coaling upstream at Rosta. The weather was as foul as ever, but
during the tinge of daylight we shoved off and hoped to make
the trip in about three hours. We made reasonable progress until
we got into the neighbourhood of Veliki Point, which is one of
those magnetic rocks which sends a compass crazy. I knew from
previous experience that my compass would swing off as much
as 70 degrees in this vicinity. If one could see the shore all was
well, but just when we reached Veliki down came the fog and I
couldn't see a thing. I took *Lady M* about a cable's length to the
starboard side of the channel and dropped the hook. I couldn't

see the shore but the echo-sounder told me we were in reasonably deep water. The fog persisted for five days, during which time we saw nothing but drifting banks of vapour and the ominous black shapes of itinerant merchant ships. We remained in sea watches and rang the ship's bell at two-minute intervals for five days and nights.

Apart from the fog, heavy snow was falling and the ship was a mass of icicles and drifts. We rigged a blue lamp as an anchor light, and this shed a weird glimmer over the foredeck. From time to time we could hear the moaning of sirens as the ships tried to grope their way down-channel. If they appeared to be getting too close we turned on our searchlight and signal projectors, and blew 'U' on *Lady M*'s siren, meaning in the international code—'You are standing into danger'.

During these days I got the impression that we might easily have strayed into another world—a world which was lit only by a ghostly blue star, where darkness reigned. I remembered a play called *Outward Bound* in which the characters were 'all dead', and I wondered if we had all died in some unaccountable way and were serving our time in hell. I began to speculate whether we had been there for days or years. The crew moved like phantoms about the decks, swathed in bundles of clothing, the ship's bell clanged incessantly and the snow fell with the relentlessness of an advancing army. I was lost; short of coal, food and water. A passage in the *Arctic Pilot* read that at this time of year such fogs often persisted for a month.

During this imprisonment I had plenty of time for reading but little to read—I was sick of the *Arctic Pilot*. All I had with me were copies of Belloc's *Cautionary Tales, The New Arabian Nights* and *The Last Enemy* by Richard Hillary. I think it was the thought of Hillary returning to the battle after he had been burnt and shot down in flames which decided me to move *Lady M*.

We got round Veliki Point, but after that the fog thickened and we steamed blindfold. We missed ships, the shore and a wharf by inches. More than half-frozen both in body and mind, I took *Lady M* alongside the Rosta coal-wharf.

Coaling took nearly a week and our crew had to do it themselves. I signed the Russian receipt for the coal, in complete ignorance. I had also to sign six copies. When I asked why, the Russian said you might swindle two or three people, but not six!

Whether it was due to drinking infected water, the cold or exhaustion, I don't know, but it was at Rosta I had another bout of Murmansk fever, which laid me out for a week. Apart from running a high temperature, I was as sick as a dog and had dysentery as well. The result was I began to get weak.

Meanwhile, our main vacuum pump had cracked up, and so had the anchor winch, so I took *Lady M* up to Murmansk to try to get some repairs done to the ship and to myself. We tied up alongside a British merchant ship, and her master, Captain Thompson, was very kind to us, providing food and some trustworthy water. I took to my bunk again, and on emerging some days later in answer to a request from Thompson to have a drink, was surprised to hear we had been asked to go to a Russian banquet. I went back to my ship and found the following invitation in Russian and English:

> Representative of the State Defence Committee of the U.S.S.R. Mr. I.D. Papanin and Representative of the People's Commissariat for Foreign Trade of the U.S.S.R. Mr. S.S. Potchenko, kindly invite you to the
> ### DINNER PARTY
> devoted to the safe arrival of the Convoy with ammunition for the Red Army at the Port of Murmansk.
>
> The Dinner will take place at the Hotel Arctic on January 17th 1943, at 19 p.m.

Apparently the Russian authorities in Moscow—or possibly 'Uncle Joe' Stalin himself—had decided to do something about the Murmansk and Archangel convoys and had organized a banquet to celebrate the safe arrival of the last convoy. Invitations had been sent to all the commanding officers of the escort force—including Captain Sherbrooke. The masters of the merchant ships had also been invited, together with our Russian naval staff. Captain Papanin and Mr. Potchenko had been sent up from Moscow, and so had a great deal of food and wine. But what the organizers of this party had not realized was that the merchant ships were strung out over the twenty miles from Kidden Island to Murmansk, with no possible transport, and that the ships of the Royal Navy were either anchored in Polyarnoe or at Vaenga Bay. *Lady M* was tied up at Murmansk at this time and so was Thompson's ship.

On the night of the party, which was 17th January 1943, the fog which had plagued us the week before came back so thickly that anybody who didn't happen to have been at Murmansk was out of the game. I went along with Thompson to the Arctic Hotel, although I was not feeling like going to a banquet, let alone a Russian one. In fact I crawled out of my bunk with the greatest effort.

Captain Papanin is, of course, a very distinguished explorer and, among other things, he has made a study of the drift of the Polar ice flow. While on this Arctic expedition, he took his ship right up into the ice in summer and remained frozen in all winter, eventually finishing up somewhere near Greenland the following summer.

I was delighted to have the chance of meeting such a man. Potchenko is also a man of great personal charm and energy, and it was he who welcomed us to the dinner party.

The company gathered in the foyer of the hotel, which was bare of furniture, but contained a brazier—such as you have on a racecourse at home on a cold day—which was crowded round, trying to thaw out. On entering, we were announced by a girl interpreter, who had been dolled up for the occasion but only succeeded in looking like a juvenile charlady. We were then led up to Captain Papanin, Mr. Potchenko and the Lord Mayor of Murmansk, who stood on a sort of raised dais (made of wooden crates marked 'Libby's Condensed Milk'). However, to celebrate this festive occasion, behind the platform someone had rigged up the Red Flag and the Union Jack, which I need hardly say was upside down. There was no American flag.

We were offered cigarettes, but there was no sign of anything to drink. After about half an hour (kick-off was supposed to be at 7 p.m.) I looked around and noticed that the Russian port officials were present in force and that some of our naval staff had appeared. A fair number of the masters of the merchant ships had arrived, but no escort commanding officers other than myself had turned up. I kept looking to see if any of the others had been able make the journey. As things were now, the Russians thought I was a 'Mr. Ogdel'—whatever that meant—and I needed R.N. support.

While I was ruminating on these rather disturbing thoughts and also suffering from nausea, the whole party was ushered into another room. This room was as bleak as the foyer, but contained a long wooden trestle table upon which stood glasses and the sort of water decanters one sees at home in railway trains. There were two other tables which had tablecloths upon them and which were loaded with red and black caviare—the Russians prefer the red caviare—smoked fish, pickled sunflower seeds, cucumbers, cold sturgeon, yak and hot potatoes. We were not asked to sit down, as there were no chairs, but the company waded into the food and of course the railway decanters contained best Russian vodka.

After about an hour, when the assembled company had thawed out and become quite talkative, to my astonishment we were ushered into a third room for dinner. This was a masterpiece of improvisation. I should tell you that the Arctic Hotel, being made of concrete, was the only building in the town which was semi-intact and had a roof over it, but I was not expecting to see the dining-room decorated with fairy lights and palm trees!

This time we sat down and were served with a dinner which might have made the Savoy Hotel envious—soup, fish, meat (veal), cheese, etc. We drank, besides vodka, Caucasian white wines, champagne from Georgia and brandy from the Balkans.

You may think it strange that I remember all this so accurately, but you would have done so too if you hadn't had a square meal for months. I have always been told that when the Russians throw a party they do things in a big way, and on this occasion they certainly did. I only wished I had been feeling better and had been able to enjoy this feast. As it was, I had some vodka, because about every five minutes Captain Papanin's interpreter rose to his feet and said: 'Captain Papanin has a word. Permit me...to ask you...to raise your glasses...and drink...to...the Krasni Army...the U.S.S.R... the Russian Navy...' and so on. We would then all stand up and pour a glass of vodka straight down the hatch—for it is considered bad manners in Russia if you sip a toast. By the time it came to the main speeches of the evening, Captain Papanin had had a lot of words and through a delightful haze I heard Commander Dixon, the Senior British Naval Staff Officer present, making a speech about the Royal Navy's part in these convoys, and saying how sorry he was that Captain Sherbrooke, V.C., was not able to be at the dinner, and that the fog had made it impossible for other senior commanding officers to attend. Too bad, I thought, trying to remember how many vodkas I had drunk. Commander Dixon ended what up to this moment had been a masterly oration by saying that in view of Sherbrooke's absence, Lieutenant Ogden, of H.M.S. *Lady Madeleine*, would respond to the toast of 'The Royal Navy'. Dixon then made violent signs for me to get up and make a speech. This wasn't too easy. I mean the getting-up part of it, not to mention trying to make a speech, I was rather surprised to find a strange man alongside me too, and thought he might be trying to help me get up. It turned out to be the interpreter. The chap who had spent the evening saying, 'Permit me...to ask you...', etc.

I've very little idea of what I said, excepting that I apologized for being such a poor substitute for Captain Sherbrooke and the rest of the R.N. escort commanders. I said I was the wrong man for the job, as I was only a R.N.V.R. Lieutenant. I also said, what is absolutely true, that the courage and endurance shown by the merchant ships is what mattered most. So, on behalf of the escort, I gave the party the toast of 'The American and British Merchant Navies'. The interpreter wasn't going to miss a chance like this, so I heard him say, 'Captain Ogden has a word...permit me...to ask you...to raise your glasses...and drink to...the Russian Merchant Navy!' I sat down, realizing that as a diplomat I was a failure. When after a lot more words the party broke up, I was taken into yet another room to have coffee, more brandy and cigars with Papanin, Potchenko and other high Russian officials. None of them spoke English, so I was in the hands of an interpreter. The upshot of this private meeting was that nothing I could say through the interpreter would convince them that I wasn't a Senior Escort Commander—the appearance of anybody else would have been an insult to them. In this confusion I was addressed as Captain Ogden, R.N., and have a hazy recollection that I was made a Hero of the Soviet Union 3rd Class. Long after midnight I found myself steering a most unsteady course for my Sea Lady.

M y health wasn't improved by this party, and the next day I was out of the hunt. While lying alongside the wharf, there had been 48 degrees of frost, and this accounted for the water-tanks, the heads, guns and winches getting frozen up. It also explained why, when I sent for a cup of tea to be sent up to the bridge, as I turned it over it fell on to the deck in a solid mass. It was clearly time I learnt something about the war.

When I said I took *Lady M* and myself up to Murmansk 'to get some repairs done to both of us', she was luckier than I was. The result of my visit to our M.O. was that for some inexplicable reason he arranged for me to go into the Russian hospital at Vaenga Bay. I suppose he had no idea what was the cure for Murmansk fever, from which I was suffering, and thought that perhaps the Russian doctors might know the answer. I vaguely remember going there under my own steam and being put on to a wooden rack. There was a Russian soldier, fully clothed, above me and something swathed in bloody bandages below me. I was delirious by now and the whole thing is like a bad dream. How long I stayed there and what—if anything—was done to me, I don't know. When one is close to death one floats about in space—one has moments of vivid consciousness, the rest of the time it is like being drunk.

It was Skipps who saved me. One day when I was dreaming about Sally I saw his honest weather-beaten face mixed up with hers. He shook me gently and made sure I could understand what he was telling me. The gist of this was that he had brought with him two bottles—one was full of some white sticky liquid and the other was whisky. He told me to try to drink both during the night, and that he had arranged for Geoff and some hands from my ship to come and take me away the next day. I understood what he had said, but drifted off into a trance and do not remember his leaving me. I did, however, manage to carry out his instructions, and, sure enough, next day my boys turned up. They wrapped me up in bear-skins and strapped me to a sledge which they pulled through the ice and snow back to *Lady M*. Whether it was the relief of being back in my own ship or Dr. Drake's medicine I don't know, but within a day or two I began to recover. Skipps came to see me and produced some mail from home. This was a lovely surprise so I crawled out of my bunk and had a 'word' or two with Skipps. Amongst other things, I got a letter, a lovely Christmas cake, lots of magazines, books, records and Christmas decorations from Sally. She had re-addressed some of the food parcels sent to her from American admirers without opening them and you would be surprised if you knew what else I found inside those parcels other than food! I was annoyed I couldn't eat the cake, but between doses of bismuth, sodium bicarbonate, magnesia and aspirin, I read the books and studied the magazines. For once the pictures in the American periodicals of tables groaning with luscious food nauseated me.

It is surprising how quickly the light starts sneaking back, and towards the end of January we had about an hour's clear daylight, which was preceded by a soft pink flush that dimmed the cold stars. In clear weather Arctic stars shine with an intensity which gives you the idea that they are tiny magnesium flares. I enjoyed these first hours of daylight, and felt a little like a moth coming out of its cocoon. But no sooner was there light than over came the German bombers. They succeeded in sinking six merchant ships which were anchored in the inlet and which had survived the perilous voyage to north Russia—a tragic anticlimax.

I must say I got a terrific shock in one of these raids. We were closed up at action stations, lying to our anchor in Vaenga Bay. The pattern was the same as usual—German bombers at high altitude, the Ruski A.A. barrage, fighters weaving about the sky and ships firing if any bomber got within their range. Suddenly I saw a plane go into a dive from about 20,000 ft. and, watching him down, I got the impression he was diving at *Lady M*. I heard that well-known screech, but didn't see or hear any bombs. I couldn't understand it. We were at anchor and my heart came into my mouth when this plane plunged into the sea with a shriek and a sizzle 20 ft. away from *Lady M*. We got slightly wet, that was all. I don't know to this day if it was a Jerry or a Russian plane; things like that just don't matter in Vaenga Bay.

Some days later I was ordered to collect mail and food from Polyarnoe and to distribute it to the escorts. This meant a day or two steaming about the inlet, and as the weather was bad and I was ill, I took a Russian pilot on board. In the smoking fog we set out for Polyarnoe and lost ourselves, for the beacon which normally marks the channel 'happened' to be out (so typically Russian) and so we had to feel our way, which meant one might go aground at any minute.

Having collected the mail and food from Polyarnoe, we spent the next day distributing it. About 1800 the following day, in thick fog, we steamed up the Kola Inlet and I was very glad I had the Russian pilot with me. Just above a place called Solni Island there is an alteration of course to port, and the pilot had just put *Lady M* on her new course when I saw some lights ahead of us. I pointed this out to the pilot, and Geoff, who was on the bridge, very sensibly said it was probably a Russian merchant ship, it being known that some were expected. From the course we were on I could see a mast-head light and a green. The pilot appeared undecided, and as the C.O. is always responsible for his ship, pilot or no pilot, I gave the order hard a-port and full ahead. Just as *Lady M* began to respond, the bow wave of a destroyer appeared amidships. Her stern could not have been more than a hundred yards away. She was travelling at speed and we were broadside on to her. The Russian pilot gave one despairing cry and fled from the bridge. The position looked quite hopeless, we were on a collision course and were going to be sliced in half. I went hard a-starboard. Geoff and I stood motionless, wondering if *Lady M*'s stern, which was filled with depth-charges, could swing clear in time, or whether we were going to be rammed.

Me: 'It's too late—we've had it.'

Geoff: 'We might do it.'

Me: 'Midships. Full ahead.'

Geoff: 'They're full astern now.'

Me: 'We're by.'

The destroyer turned out to be H.M.S. *Forester*. She had been doing 23 knots. I knew her C.O. well and when we met some time later he told me that after a spell at sea he couldn't wait to get back to base. After *Forester*'s adventures with the *Edinburgh* and the *Trinidad* this little contretemps was chicken feed, but it nearly put paid to *Lady M*. I was certainly finding out about the war.

I had a lot of difficulty in consoling our Ruski pilot, who considered he was to blame, but having done so it still turned out to be a black evening for *Lady M*, as, having had one escape, we next met the expected Russian merchant convoy and got ourselves tangled up with them. When we got clear we had lost our bearings and the pilot suggested going out to sea. I was not keen on that idea, as my only ambition was to turn in as soon as possible, so we staggered about the inlet for a few more hours and eventually succeeded in getting into a Russian Merchant Navy base, which I had never heard of, and for all I know may never have existed.

On 27th January 1943 I attended a conference for homeward-bound convoy R.A.52, which *Lady M* was to sail with. The Commodore was Captain Melhuish, who had been with J.W.51B in Sherbrooke's battle. One couldn't help admiring this tough, quiet Scotsman, who radiated confidence and courage. There were only eleven merchant ships this time and quite a powerful escort, so the chances were we would not have a rough time, excepting from the weather. The Germans very sensibly never seriously attacked ships in ballast, so we all left the conference in good heart and thinking how nice it would be to get home again.

We sailed on 29th January and arrived in home waters on 8th February. There is not much to tell about this convoy, as it was comparatively unmolested by the enemy, and, more surprising still, the weather was moderate. I, personally, was getting very near the end of my tether and still suffering from fever and dysentery, but the thought of getting home and out of the cold shadow of the north kept me up and about—it was too cold to sleep much, anyway.

On 3rd February, at 1900, a ship was torpedoed just ahead of us. We went to her assistance and found her sinking by the stern, which is a good way for a ship to sink, if sink she must, because it makes the launching of life-boats easier. On this occasion none of her crew even got wet. They were not in their life-boats more than ten minutes, and it might have been an exercise. I picked up the captain and many of the crew and *Northern Wave* picked up the remainder. Later we were able to check up, and found that no life had been lost at all. The captain had seen the torpedoes and altered course accordingly, but the ship had not responded quickly enough to get clear and the torpedoes had entered No.6 hold, which was empty.

I believe that our survivors were rather disappointed they had not had more of an exciting time. Their American life-saving gear was so good and so watertight we had to take a knife and literally cut them out of it. We found that we had also collected a U.S. naval officer, who made himself very useful, and doubled up the watch. The captain was a fine man, who had been at sea all his life, and had been torpedoed twice previously. One day when we were sitting in my cabin he rather shook me by enquiring if he could ask me a rather personal question. 'Anything you like,' I said. 'Well,' said the captain, taking out his teeth and putting them on the table, 'what did you pay for your teeth and where did you get them?...I paid 250 dollars for these.' 'Mine came with the body,' I said rather lamely, realizing that I must be looking a good sixty years old. Now I knew about the war.

*L*ady M was ordered to land her survivors at Belfast, and a signal had been made to the base that I was to go into hospital on our arrival. Steaming up the Lough gave me a strange sensation. It was at Belfast two years ago I had taken over the command of my Sea Lady and now I felt we were going to part company for ever. We had lived an exciting life together and I had got to love her. The parting was going to be a sad business, but I doubted if she would ever desert me and go to North Africa.

When I finally tied up *Lady M* in Pollock Dock, where I had first found her, and said those time-honoured words, 'Finished with the main engines', Squires, as usual, appeared on the bridge with a tumbler full of whisky. This man had been my friend and companion for two years and I can never thank him enough. I drank the whisky and went to my cabin, where I literally fell down. I was completely exhausted, but happy that I had brought *Lady M* back to port, and now, as I knew I was going into hospital the next day, my worries were ended, at least I thought they were.

While lying on the floor with Whiskers and Roubles, who were clearly anxious about my condition, I thought to myself what a miracle it was that *Lady M* and I had together taken part in a very tough contest and that we had never been seriously hit and had not lost the life of one of the crew in two years of active service, though others had died on *Lady M*'s decks. After a while, all three of us went to sleep.

I was awakened by Geoff, who seemed a little surprised to find me curled up on the floor of my cabin, but he gave me a hand and got me into my chair. He told me that if I felt strong enough the crew wanted to have one last sing-song before the ambulance arrived to take me away. We split a bottle of whisky together and I went down into the seamen's mess. I can never forget the men who had sailed with me for two years in *Lady M*. I don't have to tell you who they were because if you have read this story you will know them.

The coxswain opened up the rum and the ship's band played our favourite tunes. We sang 'Goodbye, old ship of mine', which brought tears to my eyes.

Geoff was leaving *Lady M* to take a long-overdue command of his own, and the whole ship's crew were being paid off. It was journey's end for all of us. I gave Whiskers to Squires and Roubles to

Donald, explaining he would be fun for the young 'un. I put Sally's silver slipper in my overcoat pocket.

When the time came for me to go, supported by Donald and Squires, I was piped off my Sea Lady for the last time.

EPILOGUE

Look to this Day,
For it is Life;
The Very Life of Life;
In its brief Course
Lie all The Verities
And Realities
Of your existence;
The Bliss of Growth,
The Glory of Action,
The Splendour of Beauty,
For Yesterday is but a Dream,
And Tomorrow is only a Vision,
But Today, well-lived,
Makes every yesterday
A Dream of Happiness
And every Tomorrow
A Vision of Hope.
Look well, therefore
To this Day...

Rig Veda, 3000 B.C. (*circa*)

THE RUSSIAN ARCTIC CONVOY MUSEUM PROJECT

The importance of highlighting the legacy of the WWII Arctic Convoys is central to the project plans for a Russian Arctic Convoy Museum on the shores of Loch Ewe, in Aultbea, Wester Ross, Scotland. Loch Ewe was where almost half of the convoys to Russia began their perilous journeys between 1941-1945. Over 3,000 men lost their lives in the convoys, 104 ships were sunk.

The Arctic Convoys of WWII were Britain's means of sending vital supplies and war materials to northern Russia (then part of the Soviet Union). Protected by Royal Navy warships, merchant vessels sailed from British ports to the harbours of Archangel and Murmansk. Although hazardous, this was the shortest route by which Britain could supply Russia. For Prime Minister Churchill, these supplies were a vital demonstration of Allied solidarity. He called the Arctic Convoys "the worst journey in the world".

The Museum Project is a key part in the Aultbea Regeneration Plan, together with a new Community Centre, to help bring much needed employment and income potential to the area whose community gave so much support to the war effort in this North West Highland anchorage for the Arctic Convoys. The aim of the project is to create a lasting legacy for all those who took part in the acts of heroism and extreme physical endurance that were the WWII's Arctic Convoys. The British Government have now awarded an Arctic Star medal to all those that took part. The Museum will continue to honour these great men - it is hoped to achieve this within the lifetime of some of the few remaining veterans. Go to **www.russianarcticconvoymuseum.co.uk** for more information on the project and how to donate.

c/o 20 Mellon Charles, Aultbea, Wester Ross IV22 2JN